ART SCHOOL

DRAWING

Step-by-step teaching through inspirational projects

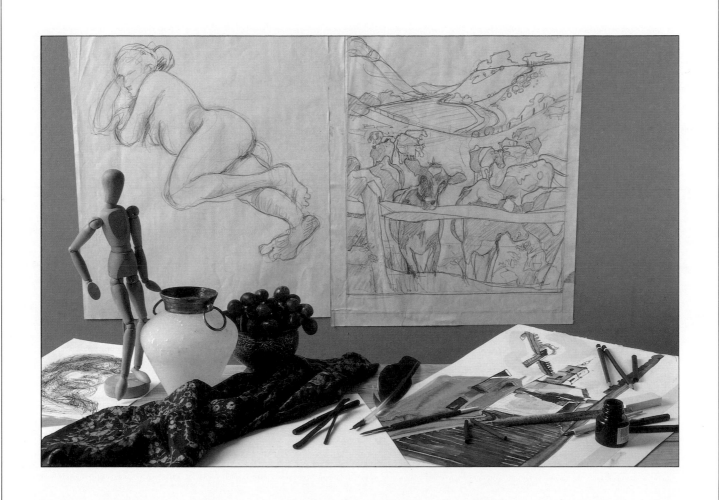

HAZEL HARRISON

LORENZ BOOKS

This edition published by Lorenz Books
27 West 20th Street, New York, NY 10011

LORENZ BOOKS are available for bulk purchase for sales promotion
and for premium use. For details, write or call the sales director,
Lorenz Books, 27 West 20th Street, New York, NY 10011;
(800) 354-9657

Lorenz Books is an imprint of
Anness Publishing Inc.

Publisher: Joanna Lorenz
Project Editor: Samantha Gray
Designer: Michael Morey
Photographers: Paul Forrester and John Freeman

Previously published as part of a larger compendium,
How to Paint and Draw

© Anness Publishing Limited 1996
Updated © 2000
1 3 5 7 9 10 8 6 4 2

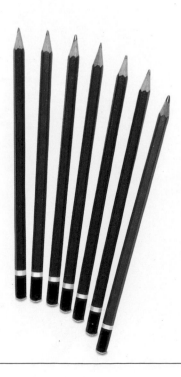

CONTENTS

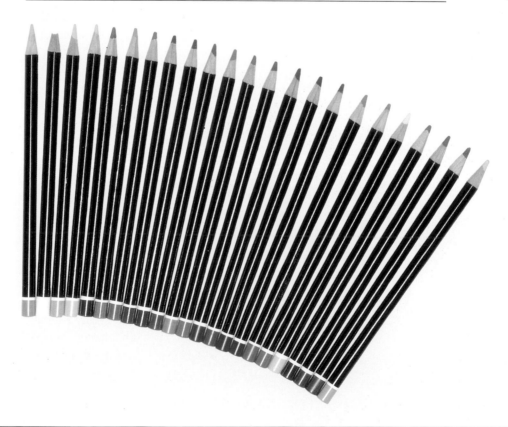

Introduction
DRAWING

It is not easy to define the word "drawing" because it embraces a wide range of related but different activities. At its simplest it can be described as marks made on a sheet of paper, and in this sense it is one of the most basic of all human activities. Young children enjoy scribbling with a pencil or crayon as soon as they have developed sufficient manual dexterity to grip the implement, and long before they consider relating what they are doing to the world they see around them.

This enjoyment of the lines and marks made by various drawing implements is an important factor in all drawing, and paramount in the work of some artists – the modern Swiss painter and draughtsman, Paul Klee, described his drawing as "taking a line for a walk". For most artists, however, drawing also performs a descriptive function: it is a direct response to the visual stimuli of our surroundings.

LEARNING TO DRAW
Drawing is often regarded as a special gift, and it is true that there are people who seem

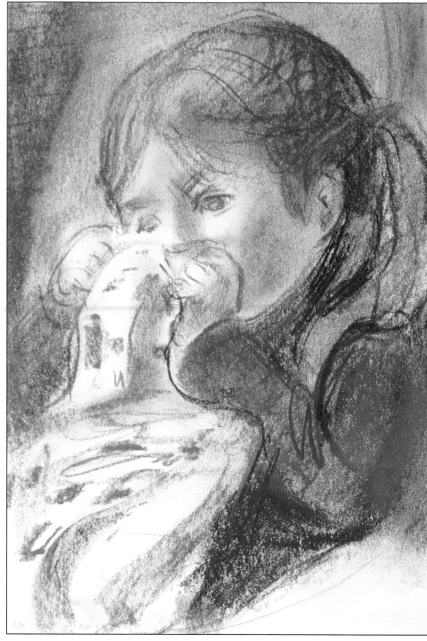

TED GOULD
CLAIRE
(Above) *Pastel is a lovely medium for portraiture and is particularly well-suited to studies of children, as it creates gentle effects in keeping with the subject. On the face and clothing the artist has applied the colours lightly, rubbing them slightly into the paper to create soft blends, reinforced with crisp linear drawing.*

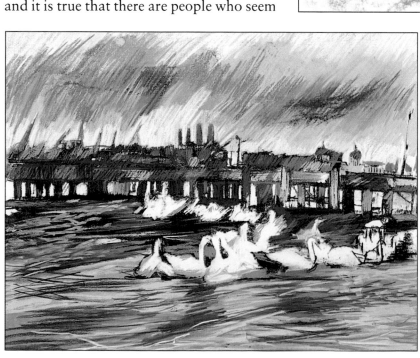

PIP CARPENTER
SWANS ON THE THAMES
(Left) *Pastel need not be a soft and delicate medium; it is extremely versatile and responsive to the artist's visual interests and ways of working. Here the artist has created energetic and exciting effects in the picture by laying heavy strokes of unblended colour, using the tip of the pastel stick.*

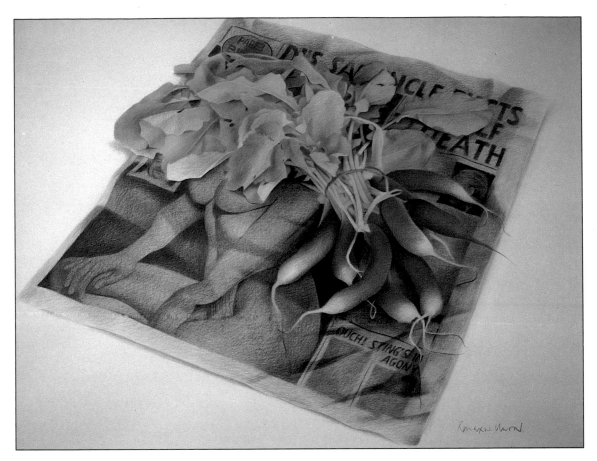

ROBERT
MAXWELL WOOD
YESTERDAY'S
NUDES, RADISHES
(Left) *In his picture, this
artist uses coloured
pencil in a completely
different way to John
Townend (below). He
achieves meticulous
detail and considerable
depth of colour with
successive layers of
coloured pencil, using
a delicate shading
technique so that almost
no lines are visible.*

to be able to draw quite effortlessly. Yet
drawing, like writing, is a skill which can be
acquired; if the motivation is there, most
people can learn to draw accurately. In the
past, students were taught to draw in a
certain way, with the emphasis on
mastering a specific set of techniques, but
this ignored the essential fact that drawing
is first and foremost about seeing.

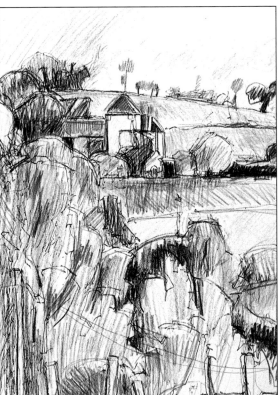

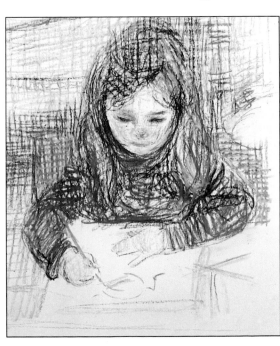

TED GOULD
GIRL SKETCHING
(Right) *Wax crayon is a
less subtle drawing
medium than pastel, but
it has the advantage of
not smudging and is thus
useful for sketchbook
drawings and quick
impressions. In this
lively drawing, the artist
has built up the forms
and colours with a
network of loose
hatching and cross-
hatching lines.*

JOHN TOWNEND
SUMMER VIEW BEYOND THE POOL
(Above) *This artist works out of doors directly from
his subject, and finds coloured pencil ideal for his
particular approach. He uses the medium in a free and
instinctive manner, with bold hatching lines varying
in direction according to the forms he is describing.*

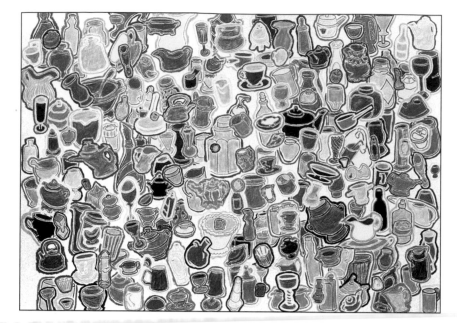

DAVID CUTHBERT
POLLY WANTS A POT
(Left) *In this delightful and inventive drawing,
coloured pencil has been pressed heavily into the
paper to achieve areas of heavy, almost flat colour.
The two-dimensional pattern element is stressed by
the use of coloured outlines.*

Although technical skill is important, it is
not the first stage in learning how to draw,
as it is pointless to develop techniques in a
void. You may produce beautifully even
lines of hatching and cross-hatching but still
find that you have failed in the primary task
of drawing, which is to describe the subject
to your own satisfaction. Such failures are
nearly always the direct result of poor
observation, not of inadequate technique.

It sounds easy enough to say that if you
want to learn how to draw all you need to

do is to look at things, but it is not that
simple, because you have to learn to look in
a certain way, analytically and objectively.
This can be a surprisingly hard skill to
master, as it involves looking at a subject
with a fresh eye every time, abandoning
preconceptions. Our brains are cluttered
with information which can be actively
unhelpful in the context of drawing, leading
us to quite the wrong conclusions – we tend
to draw what we know from experience
rather than what we see with our own eyes.

PAUL BARTLETT
STILL LIFE WITH
MAN-MADE AND
NATURAL OBJECTS
*A combination of pastel
and pastel pencil has
been used for this
exploration of shapes
and forms. The light
brown paper chosen by
the artist has allowed
him to build up both
highlights and shadows
with light overlays of
white and brown pastel.
It has also given a subtle
touch of colour to
what is essentially a
monochrome drawing.*

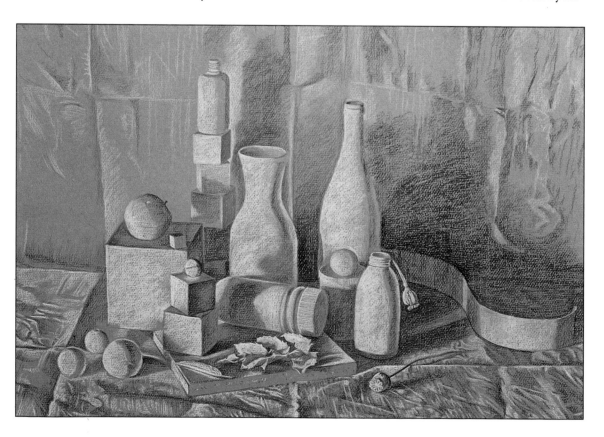

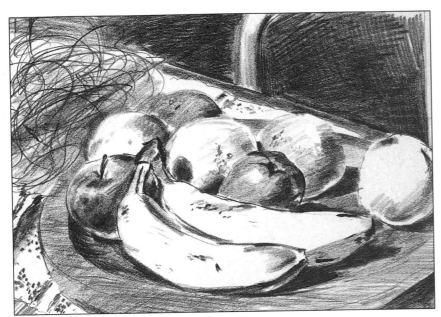

GERRY BAPTIST
BANANAS AND OTHER FRUIT
(Left) *This lovely drawing is also a study of form, done in very soft pencil, which blunts easily and thus provides broader, bolder effects than hard or medium pencil. Both this and Bartlett's still life are carefully composed, showing that a drawing in monochrome can make as complete a statement as a coloured drawing or painting.*

PAUL BARTLETT
SELF PORTRAIT
(Below) *A comparison between this drawing and Gerry Baptist's demonstrates the versatility of the pencil. Here the effect is almost photographic in its minute attention to detail and texture and its subtle gradations of tone.*

A classic example is relative size, which can be hard to get right, particularly when you are drawing familiar objects. If you place one large object on a table with a much smaller one in front of it, the chances are that you will make the larger one too large because of your prior knowledge of it. But in fact the effects of perspective will have caused it to "shrink", so that it may be smaller than the object nearer to you. The only way to approach drawing a known subject, whether it be a portrait, an apple on

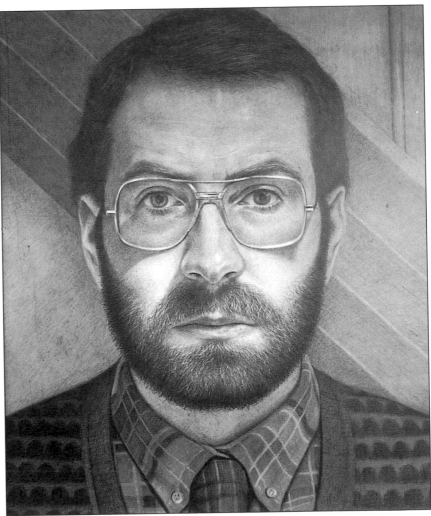

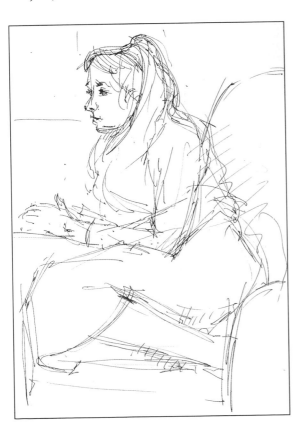

TED GOULD
GIRL IN AN ARMCHAIR
(Left) *Pen and ink can achieve intricate and elaborate effects, but it is also a lovely medium for rapid line drawings. In this figure study the artist has caught the essentials of the pose in a few pen strokes, sometimes superimposing lines where the first drawing was incorrect or needed clarifying.*

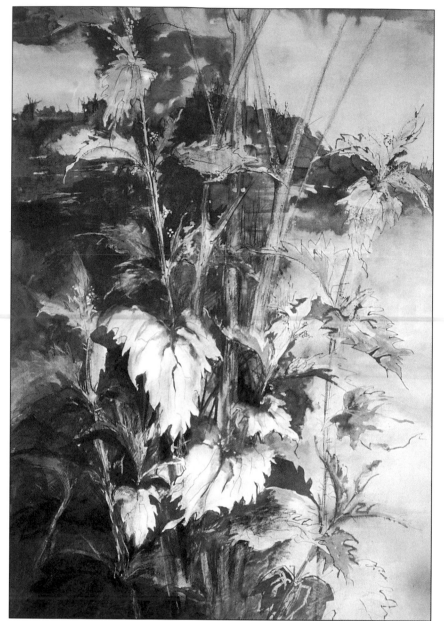

JOHN TOWNEND
SHUNTING LOCOMOTIVE AT BOW
(Below) *For this sketch, made on location, the artist has used oil pastel, an ideal medium for bold effects and quick impressions, as colours can be built up rapidly. Also, unlike soft pastel, oil pastel does not smudge and does not require fixing. The sgraffito technique has been used to add touches of linear detail to the side of the coach.*

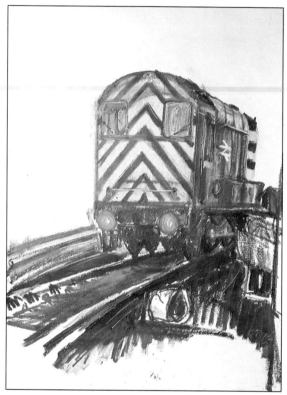

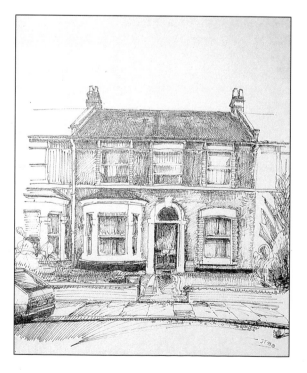

ELISABETH HARDEN
NETTLES
(Above) *The attractive combination of pen lines and washes of diluted ink (watercolour can also be used) allows tones to be built up with greater speed than is possible with line alone. Pen and wash is ideal both for broad treatments and the kind of delicate effect seen in this drawing.*

a plate or a tree, is to force yourself to abandon preconceptions by pretending to yourself that you have never seen it before. Only in this way will you be able to assess it thoroughly and draw it accurately.

DIFFERENT KINDS OF DRAWING

A drawing can be many things: it can be a few lines of "visual shorthand" in a sketchbook, made to remind the artist of some salient point in a subject; it can be a first step in painting, subsequently hidden by layers of paint and thus having no independent existence; it can be a finished work of art in its own right, planned, composed and executed with as much thought as a painting.

PIP CARPENTER
THREE FISHES
(Right) *This is also a mixed-media work, but a more unusual combination has been used: oil paint, used thinly on paper, and coloured pencils. There are no set rules about mixed-media drawing; only by experimenting will you discover which work well together and which do not.*

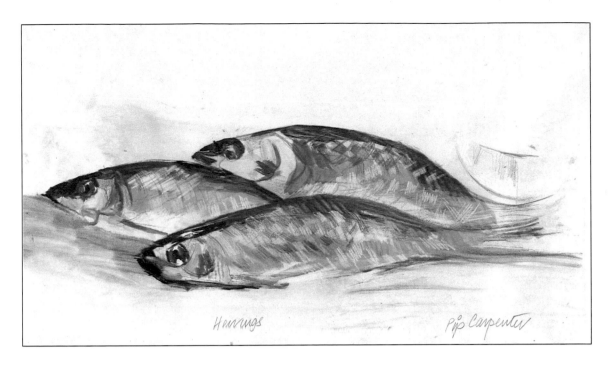

The kind of drawing you make depends on how you view the purpose of the activity – why are you drawing? You may draw simply because you love to do so, in which case, once you have mastered the "alphabet" of drawing you will find it a satisfying means of self-expression. You may have aspirations to become an illustrator, or you may simply want to improve your observational skills because you enjoy painting.

If you view drawing as a necessary foundation skill for painting, accuracy will be the main aim, and it does not matter very much which medium you use, but for those who enjoy drawing for its own sake, it is rewarding to experiment with different media. There is now a wider choice of drawing materials than ever before, from the traditional graphite pencil to a whole range of colourful and versatile pastels, coloured pencils, inks and felt-tipped pens. The word "drawing" no longer conjures up an image of timid grey pencil marks on white paper – much more exciting effects than this are achievable.

JOAN ELLIOTT BATES
WHITE VILLAGE, SOUTH SPAIN
(Right) *In this delightful drawing – which could be described equally well as a painting – the artist has used pen and ink with light washes of watercolour. These have spread the ink in places so that there is no obvious boundary between line and colour. When using a mixture of media it is important that the two work together, or the drawing will lack unity.*

JOHN TOWNEND
EAST END FAMILY HOUSE
(Opposite) *In this pen-and-ink drawing, tones have been built up by hatching and cross-hatching, a method which can create a somewhat mechanical impression, but which has been used loosely here, with the lines almost scribbled over one another in varying directions. Pen and ink is a good medium for rapid location sketches like this, as the impossibility of erasing encourages a decisive approach.*

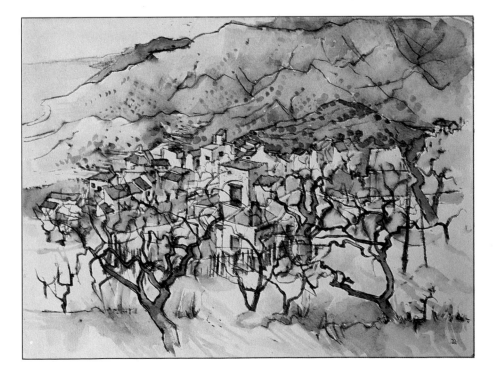

MONOCHROME DRAWING MATERIALS

Many people picture a drawing as a work in monochrome – pencil, pen and ink or charcoal. In the past most drawings were indeed in one colour or perhaps two, largely because colour drawing materials, with the exception of pastels, did not arrive on the art scene until relatively recently. Now there are a great many, which are discussed later. However, because most people begin drawing with monochrome materials we will look at these first.

PENCILS

These are the most basic of all drawing tools, as well as being one of the most sensitive and versatile. Few artists would be without a selection of pencils. Although they are sometimes incorrectly described as "lead", pencils are in fact made of graphite, a form of carbon, and began to be manufactured in the 18th century after the discovery of a deposit in the north of England. They are made in different grades, from 8B, which is very soft, to about 4H, which is much too hard for ordinary

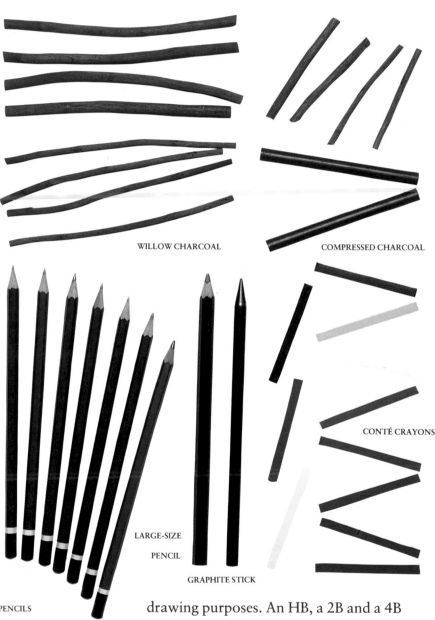

WILLOW CHARCOAL

COMPRESSED CHARCOAL

CONTÉ CRAYONS

LARGE-SIZE
PENCIL

GRAPHITE STICK

PENCILS

drawing purposes. An HB, a 2B and a 4B would provide a good selection for the beginner to practise with.

CONTÉ CRAYONS

These are square-sectioned sticks, similar to hard pastels in consistency. They are made in black, white, and a selection of "earth" colours – browns and red-browns. They are capable of much bolder effects than pencil, and are excellent both for crisp, decisive lines and for areas of solid dark tone, as they can be sharpened to a point or broken into short lengths and used sideways. The

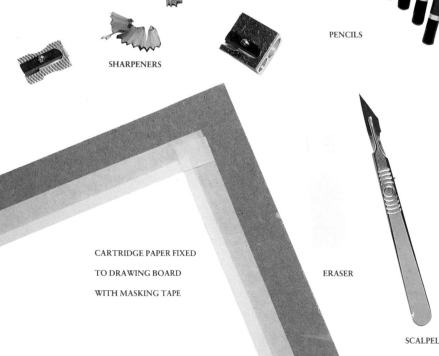

SHARPENERS

CARTRIDGE PAPER FIXED
TO DRAWING BOARD
WITH MASKING TAPE

ERASER

SCALPEL

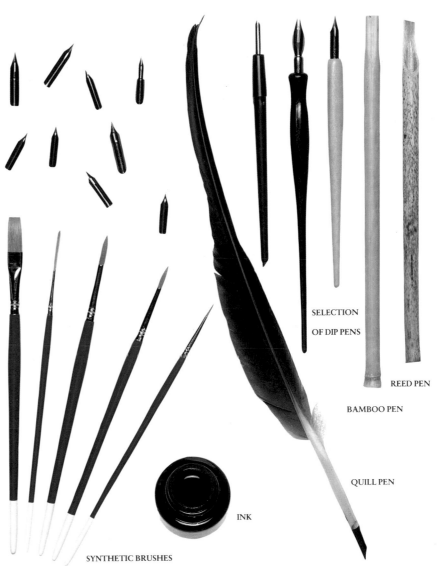

INTER-CHANGEABLE
NIBS FOR
PEN HOLDER

SELECTION
OF DIP PENS

REED PEN

BAMBOO PEN

QUILL PEN

INK

SYNTHETIC BRUSHES

only drawback is that Conté cannot be erased easily.

CHARCOAL

This is one of the most popular of all the monochrome media. Because it encourages a bold, uninhibited form of drawing, art teachers often recommend it to novices. Charcoal is made from fired twigs of wood, such as willow, and is sold in different thicknesses. It smudges easily, and corrections can be made simply by wiping it off; however, this makes it less suitable than pencil for small-scale sketchbook work.

Compressed charcoal is also available, in both stick and pencil form. This produces deeper, richer blacks than ordinary charcoal, but is less easy to erase.

PENS, INKS AND BRUSHES

There are a great many different kinds of pen, ranging from modern felt- and fibre-tips to "old-fashioned" implements such as quills and reed pens. Perhaps it is best to start with one of the inexpensive wooden or plastic handles sold with a set of various interchangeable nibs which will enable you to practise your "handwriting" in pen and ink; this type of pen may well remain a favourite item of equipment, as it does for many professional artists.

There is a variety of drawing inks on the market, but they can be divided into two basic types: water-soluble and waterproof, the latter being shellac- or acrylic-based. Water-soluble ink can be diluted with water and is therefore useful for wash drawings, where you want a range of greys as well as black. Waterproof ink should never be used in reservoir-type pens, as it clogs them up. Felt- and fibre-tipped pens are also made in waterproof and water-soluble versions – check in your art shop, as they are not

always clearly labelled. Brushes are not a necessity, but they are sensitive drawing implements, producing an expressive line.

PAPERS

The most common surface for drawing is plain white cartridge (drawing) paper. For wash drawings, make sure that you buy good-quality cartridge (drawing) paper.

Some artists prefer to use a paper with a texture for charcoal drawings. Textured paper can also be used for Conté drawings. If you want solid blacks (or browns), however, stick to smooth cartridge (drawing) paper.

ADDITIONAL EQUIPMENT

A rigid board of some kind is required to support the paper. You will also need erasers, a craft knife and a can of spray fixative if you intend to use charcoal.

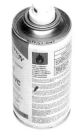

SPRAY FIXATIVE

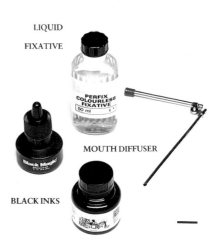

LIQUID
FIXATIVE

MOUTH DIFFUSER

BLACK INKS

PENCIL

As the pencil is such a versatile drawing implement, it allows each artist to develop his or her own "handwriting" in drawing. There are so many different ways of using pencil that no one technique or set of techniques can really be singled out as belonging particularly to this medium.

LINE AND TONE

The grade of pencil and the subject you choose to draw are both major influences on the way you use the pencil. An HB pencil, for example, gives light, fine lines, so it is not suitable for broad effects involving heavy shading and smudging methods. This relatively hard pencil would be a good choice for a subject such as flowers, where fine lines and delicate areas of tone could be built up by light shading or hatching and cross-hatching. The latter technique, which is used in all the line media, is dealt with in more detail under pen and ink.

Soft pencils, such as 6B and 8B, can create thick dark areas; indeed a drawing in soft pencil can look very similar to one in Conté crayon. These pencils are most suitable for drawings in which line plays a subsidiary role. They are ideal for rendering tonal effects, such as light and shade in a landscape or the modelling on forms – perhaps a face or figure seen in strong side-lighting. If you are drawing or sketching out of doors, rather than working from a subject that you have set up specially at home, take a good selection of pencils with you, as your initial direct response to the subject will often dictate the kind of drawing that you make.

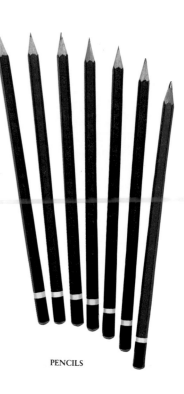

PENCILS

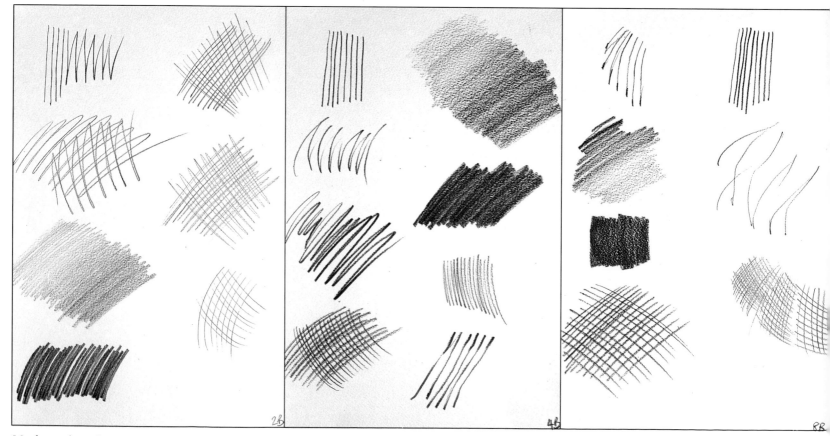

Marks made with a 2B pencil

Marks made with a 4B pencil

Marks made with an 8B pencil

FROTTAGE

This is a specialist technique which is worth knowing about. It is not restricted to pencil drawing – charcoal, Conté crayon or pastel can also be used. The term "frottage" comes from the French verb *frotter*, to rub, and the method will be familiar to anyone who has made or seen brass rubbings. A piece of paper is placed over a textured surface, or one with an incised pattern, and soft pencil is rubbed over the paper. The method is often used to create areas of pattern or texture in a drawing – for example, patterns of wood grain taken from a rough piece of timber could be incorporated into a still life. The effects which can be achieved vary according to the paper used. Brass rubbings are done on thin paper because this yields the crispest and clearest impressions; on ordinary drawing paper, pencil frottage produces a more blurred result which may suggest a texture without being specific as to its nature.

Frottage method

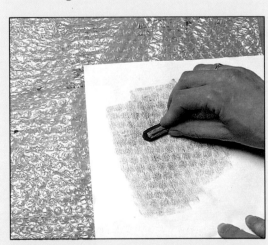

You need a soft pencil and fairly thin paper for a clear impression. Here a graphite stick (a pencil without the wooden casing) is used to take a rubbing from a piece of bubble wrap.

6 (Right) *The finished collage shows an interesting use of frottage, which can be difficult to use in a "normal" drawing.*

Collage of frottage textures

1 *A variety of frottage textures has been obtained from surfaces in the artist's home. These have been made on thin cartridge (drawing) paper, which has given good impressions; it is also easier to stick down than thick paper.*

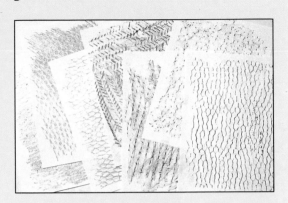

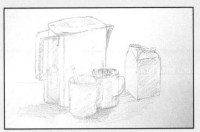

2 *A working drawing is made first to plan the composition, with light shading indicating where the dark and light tones are to be placed.*

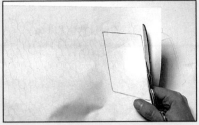

3 *A tracing has been made from the drawing, and lines are transferred to the back of each piece of paper. The first piece is cut out.*

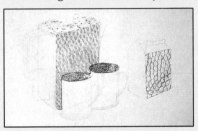

4 *The artist moves the collage pieces around for the best placing before gluing them down in their final positions.*

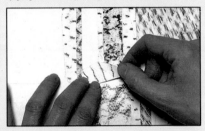

5 *At a certain point, she begins to depart from the shapes in the master drawing, letting the collage develop independently.*

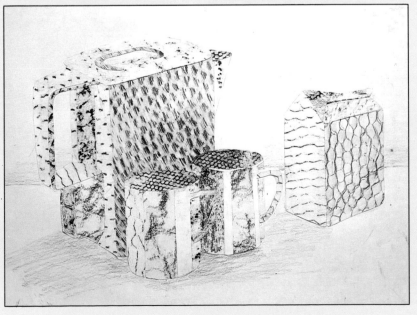

CHARCOAL

Charcoal is a wonderfully versatile medium, responsive to the slightest change in the amount of pressure applied, depending on how the stick is held. Fine sticks of willow charcoal can produce either delicate effects or tough, crisp lines resembling those in certain pencil drawings, while at the other extreme, a thick stick of charcoal or compressed charcoal used on its side allows you to build up deep, rich areas of tone.

Ordinary cartridge (drawing) paper has a smooth surface, which does not hold the charcoal well, so for drawings where tone is more important than line, you may need either to spray the work with fixative at intervals or to use a paper with more texture, such as Ingres paper, watercolour paper or recycled paper. These will grip the charcoal dust more firmly and allow you to

achieve a denser coverage. For line drawings or fine, light effects, however, cartridge (drawing) paper is ideal.

ERASING TECHNIQUES

Charcoal can be erased completely, but this is somewhat laborious and not in keeping with the boldness and immediacy of the medium; it is more usual to rub down any incorrect lines, producing an area of grey with "ghost lines" which can be drawn over. These, which are often an exciting feature of drawings in charcoal, are helpful from a practical point of view too, as it is easier to correct or amend a drawing when the wrong lines are still visible.

The ease with which charcoal can be rubbed down has given rise to an interesting technique known as "lifting out". This

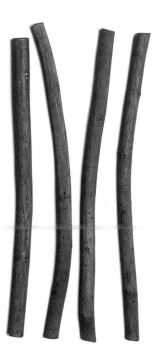

WILLOW CHARCOAL

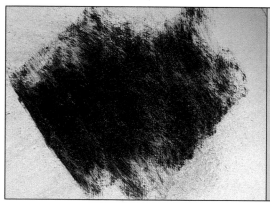
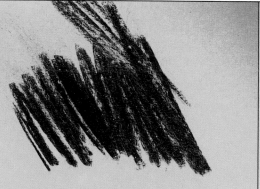
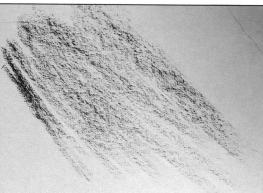

Charcoal on Ingres paper

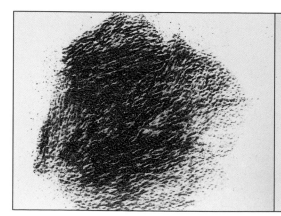
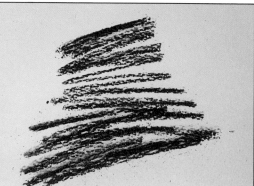
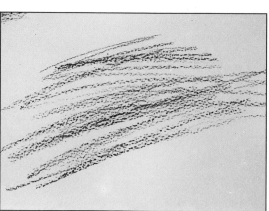

Charcoal on watercolour paper

Lifting out charcoal

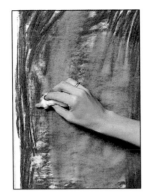 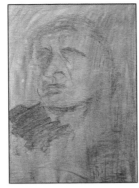 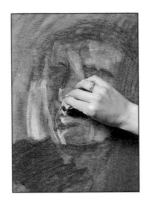 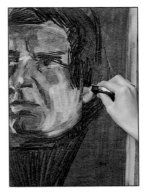 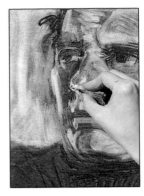

1 *Having covered a sheet of cartridge (drawing) paper with charcoal, the artist wipes it down with cotton wool (a cotton ball) to produce grey.*

2 *A rough drawing over the grey background establishes the darker tones of the picture and provides a guide for the highlights to be lifted out.*

3 *Using a putty eraser, the artist works on the main light areas of the subject, using the side of the eraser for broad strokes and the corner for finer detail.*

4 *The darker areas have been defined with further bold applications of charcoal, and the corner of the eraser is now used to create a new highlight.*

5 *For the finer details, the putty eraser is pulled into a point and used as one might use a pastel stick or pencil.*

6 (Right) *The method encourages bold drawing and dramatic, painterly effects – the lifted-out highlights look similar to brushstrokes.*

reverses the usual drawing procedure, in which the darkest tones are built up gradually; here you work from dark to light, picking out the highlights with a putty eraser. This method is often applied to figure drawing – art teachers find it encourages an unfussy approach – but any subject which has strong contrasts of tone can be drawn in this way.

The usual method is to start by covering the whole of the paper with charcoal, rub it down to produce an overall mid-grey and then make a line drawing over this. The drawing is in turn rubbed down to produce a ghost image which provides a guide for the next stage – that of lifting out the highlights. Once the main highlights are in place, the mid-tones are established by working more lightly with the eraser, after which the darks can be strengthened if necessary with further applications of charcoal. It is not as difficult as it sounds, and you can achieve quite precise effects with the putty eraser, which can be pulled into a point for fine lines and used on the flat for large areas.

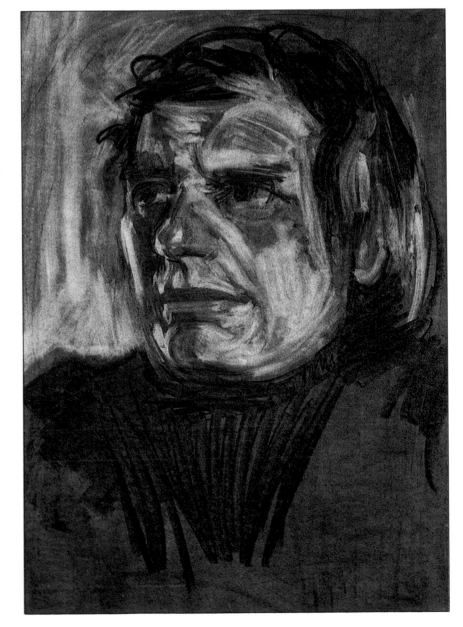

CONTÉ CRAYON

Black Conté crayons and Conté pencils give a less subtle line than charcoal or pencil, but are excellent for bold effects. Conté crayons are made from natural earth pigments held together with a binder, which makes them less crumbly than charcoal, enabling you to build up solid areas of black because the colour grips the paper more firmly. You don't usually need to fix Conté drawings, as they don't smudge easily, but it is difficult to erase mistakes cleanly. The brown and brownish-red crayons and pencils yield more delicate effects and are perhaps more sympathetic to use than the black – throughout the history of art the so-called "sanguine" (red-brown) chalks or crayons have been much favoured for portrait and figure drawings.

PAPER TEXTURE
As with charcoal drawings, the texture of the paper plays a part in the final appearance of the work, but here the smoother the paper, the darker the drawing will be. A textured surface, such as pastel paper or medium-surface watercolour paper, breaks up the strokes, allowing tiny specks of white to show through to create a slight speckling which can be highly effective in a light- or mid-toned drawing.

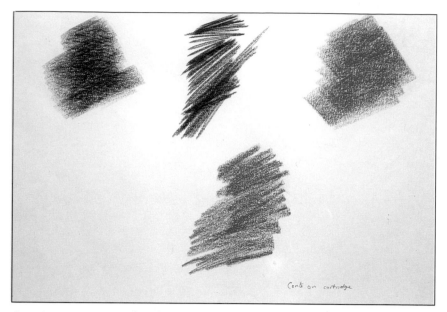

Conté crayon on cartridge (drawing) paper

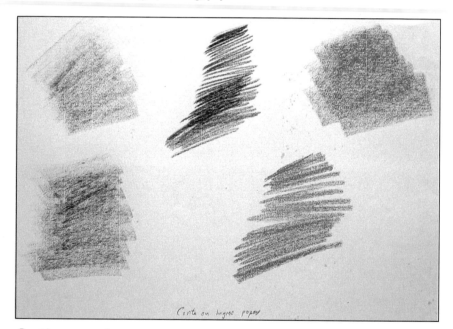

Conté crayon on Ingres paper

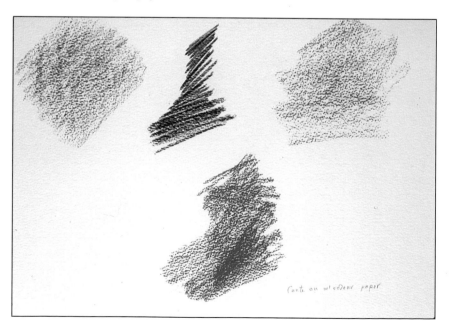

Conté crayon on watercolour paper

WORKING À TROIS COULEURS

Drawings in sanguine Conté crayons are often done on a lightly coloured paper, usually a warm cream or light brown, which enhances the rich colours. For a low-key effect, black Conté can be used on a grey or blue paper, which provides a middle tone. Such drawings can be left as they are, with only dark and mid-tones, but a traditional technique is to pick out the highlights in white Conté, using, in effect, three colours – hence *trois couleurs*. This is an excellent way to model form, and the method was extensively used by the old masters for nude studies. Areas of the paper are left uncovered, while the light and dark tones are achieved by shading with white and black (or sanguine and brown) Conté respectively. Very subtle and beautiful effects can be achieved in this way.

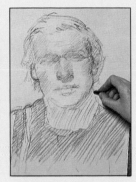

1 *The artist is working on off-white Ingres paper, and has begun the drawing in dark brown Conté crayon. She uses black to strengthen some lines slightly.*

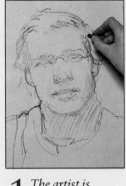

2 *A middle tone has been established with loose diagonal hatching lines of sanguine crayon; black is again used lightly on the shadowed side of the face and neck.*

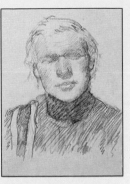

3 *The face is now beginning to take on solid, three-dimensional form, although the crayon work is still light and delicate.*

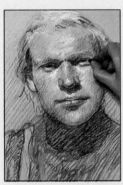

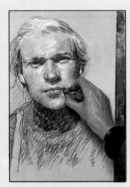

4 *Highlights have been added in white crayon, and the whole face comes alive with the definition of the eyes.*

5 *A putty eraser is used to soften the patch of dark shading at the corner of the mouth. Conté cannot be erased completely, but it can be softened and smudged.*

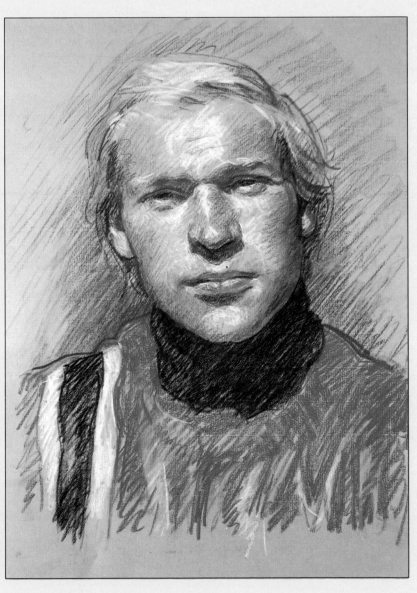

6 *(Right) The finished drawing has the look of a painting, although only three colours have been used, plus white and the colour of the paper.*

PEN & INK

The pencil was a relatively recent arrival on the art scene, but pen and ink have been with us for many centuries; in China, inks were being made as early as 2,550 BC, and in Ancient Egypt reed pens were used for both writing and drawing. Reed pens, bamboo pens and quill pens – the latter being the standard writing implement in Europe until the 19th century – are now enjoying a major artistic revival, and are well worth experimenting with. They can be bought from specialist suppliers or you can make your own, as many artists do.

However, there are also many different types of ready-made pen on the market today, all of which create different effects.

SCRIBBLE DRAWING

You can also build up tones and forms in a looser, less-organized way, by scribbling with the pen. This is a harder technique to handle than hatching and cross-hatching as it has a random quality – you must learn to let the pen do the work, moving around freely until the correct density is built up. It was a technique much used by Picasso when in revolt against traditional methods, and can give a dynamic quality to a drawing.

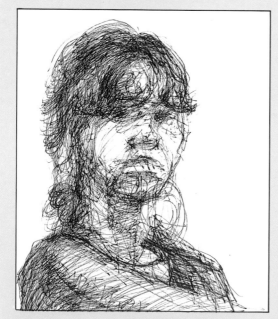

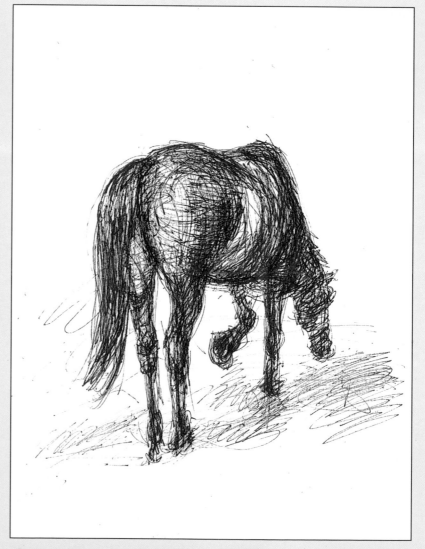

1 *A fine fibre-tipped pen has been used for this self-portrait, and the forms have been constructed in a free and spontaneous way, with the pen moving almost randomly over the paper.*

2 *Here the same technique has been used for an animal drawing. In this case the artist worked from a photograph because scribble drawing takes longer than a line sketch in pencil or charcoal, and is thus not ideal for a live, moving subject.*

HATCHING AND CROSS-HATCHING

As pen and ink is uncompromising in its linearity – you can't shade and smudge as you can with pencil and charcoal – tones must be described with a network of lines. Hatching lines are those which go in one direction, while in cross-hatching a further set of lines is made on top of those in the opposite direction. Obviously the closer together the lines are, the darker the tone will be.

These methods offer numerous possibilities, because, although the lines should be roughly parallel, they need not be straight and even. The traditional method of hatching was to use a series of slanting lines, and this is still the commonest technique, but the lines can curve slightly to follow the shape of certain objects. This can give a less-mechanical look to the finished drawing, and also helps to build up a three-dimensional impression.

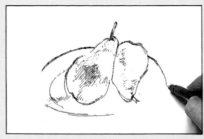

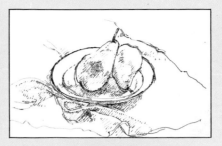

1 *The artist is using a fine, metal-pointed pen of the kind used by graphic designers, and is working on a sheet of good-quality cartridge (drawing) paper.*

2 *She will introduce more of the drapery at a later stage, but she begins with the pears on the plate. Notice how she has varied the hatching lines, from long diagonals to small dots and dashes.*

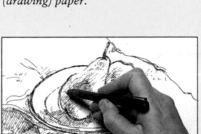

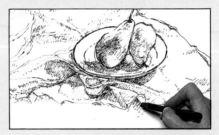

3 *The forms of the pears are built up more solidly with further hatching lines, which are denser and closer together at the centre of the pear, where there is an area of dark shadow.*

4 *With pears and plate complete, further work is then carried out on the drapery, with lightly scribbled lines deepening the shadow in the foreground.*

5 *(Right) The drawing is a convincing rendering of three-dimensional form, and the variety of different lines creates a lively effect. Although all roughly diagonal, they are only parallel and evenly spaced where the artist wanted to describe the flat plane of the table top.*

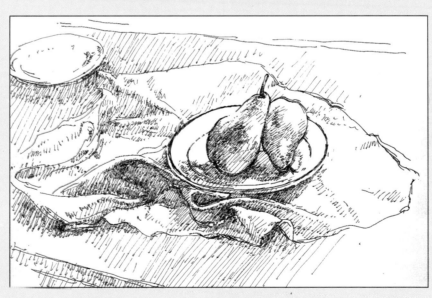

You really need to try them out to discover which ones you prefer, but fortunately most good art shops will let you do this, and provide pads of paper for scribbling on.

To some extent your choice will depend on the kind of drawing you intend to do and where you are working. For example, a fibre- or felt-tipped pen would be unlikely to provide the delicacy of line needed for a flower study, but might be ideal for quick outdoor sketches in the town or countryside, as a bottle of ink is not required. Don't neglect the possibilities of the humble ballpoint pen either – this can be a useful drawing tool, with the added advantage of being familiar to handle.

LINE & WASH

Another way to build up areas of tone in a pen-and-ink drawing is to combine the line element with washes made from diluted water-soluble ink or black watercolour. This method is used in watercolour painting, when the washes are in colour, but it is equally effective for introducing tone to monochrome drawings.

It is an attractive and enjoyable technique, allowing you to work more freely and rapidly than you can with pen alone, because you don't have to rely on the line to provide the tone. Both Rembrandt and Nicolas Poussin in the 17th century exploited line and wash with consummate skill, producing beautifully expressive drawings. The technique is closely associated with figure drawing, but it is equally suitable for other subjects, such as landscapes, urban scenes and flowers.

PENS AND PAPERS

A varied line gives the best effect, so this might be the time to try out quill, bamboo or reed pens. You can use drawing pens or felt-tips, but these tend to create a slightly rigid impression because the line is always the same thickness. Interesting effects can be created by working with a bamboo pen on a slightly textured watercolour paper, rather than cartridge (drawing) paper, as this produces a "dry", broken line.

If you intend to use a good deal of wash you may need to stretch the paper first, otherwise it could buckle under the water and spoil your work. Soak the paper in a bath for a few minutes, lift it out carefully and shake off the excess water, then place it on a drawing board and stick gumstrip (gummed brown paper tape) all around the edges, smoothing the paper with a damp sponge as you work. Leave it to dry naturally if possible; if you put it in front of

Using brush and reed pens

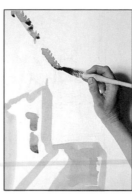
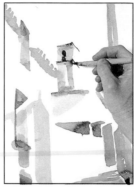
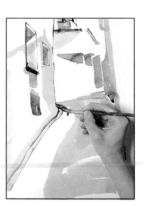

1 *This subject has contrasting areas of light and shadow, so the artist begins by working in tone, using a large soft brush and water-soluble ink.*

2 *A reed pen is used, with undiluted ink, to draw into the washes. These pens give a bolder but more sensitive line than mechanically produced drawing pens.*

3 *Line is not intended to play a dominant role, so pen and brush-work are developed at the same time, with darker washes now painted over the pen lines.*

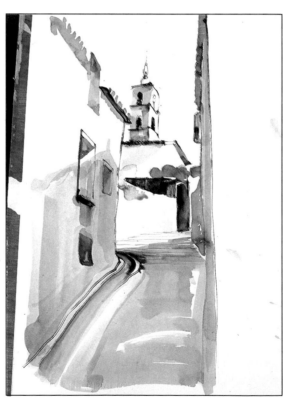

4 *The drawing is at a halfway stage, and the artist assesses it to see which areas require further definition. Notice that, because water-soluble ink has been used, the washes of diluted ink have spread and softened the pen lines.*

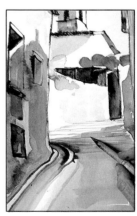

5 *The shadow on the left-hand building has been deepened with further washes, and the reed pen is used again, this time with well-watered ink, to make light lines at the top of the steps.*

the fire or use a hairdryer, the tape will dry before the paper and may tear off.

WORKING METHODS

In order to produce a well-integrated drawing, try to develop the line and wash together, rather than "filling in" a line drawing. One way to do this is to use water-soluble ink in the pen, as you can spread this with a brush and clean water in places to soften the line and then apply more washes as required. However, some artists prefer the line to remain crisp; they use waterproof ink in the pen and water-soluble ink for the washes. You can also reverse the normal procedure (which is to begin with the drawing) and lay some washes first in order to establish the tonal structure of the subject, using pen later to add details and touches of definition. This could be a particularly suitable approach for a landscape subject.

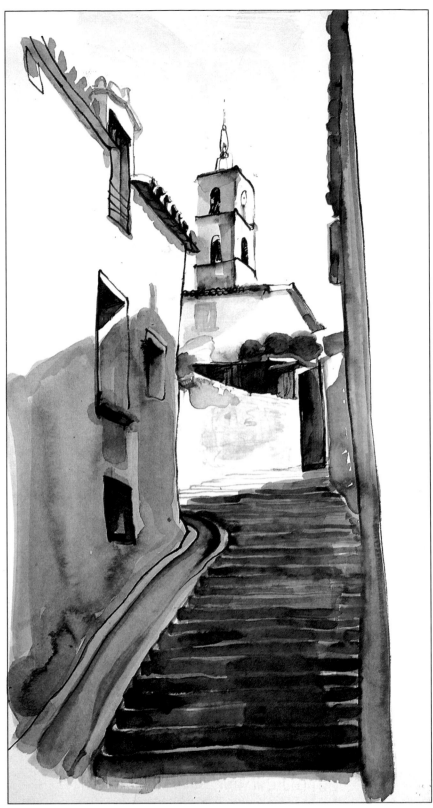

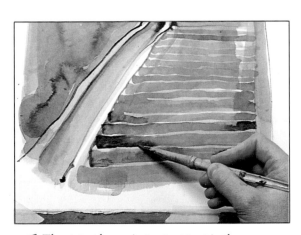

6 The steps play an important part in the composition, as they lead the eye in towards the focal point, which is the church tower, so they are defined carefully with a combination of washes and decisive pen work.

7 The bold, broad lines of the reed pen complement the loose washes to create a well-integrated drawing. At the bottom of the wall on the left, the artist has exploited one of the semi-accidental effects known as backruns, which quite often occur in wash and watercolour work, to suggest the texture of old plasterwork.

BRUSH DRAWING

In a pen-and-wash drawing, the pen provides the linear element; you can, however, dispense with the pen altogether and make drawings entirely with a brush, a method which takes you into the area of painting. The tip of a good brush can provide quite fine definition and, if this is combined with washes, the effect is similar to that of a pen-and-wash drawing but softer, and the line and tone are automatically well-integrated because the same implement has been used for both. Rembrandt made some wonderful brush-and-wash figure drawings, and the great 19th-century English landscape painter, John Constable, used the method for landscape sketches – it is particularly well suited to quick on-the-spot tonal studies.

A variant on the method is to work on dampened paper, which spreads and diffuses the washes to create soft effects, ideal for subjects such as misty landscapes and certain weather conditions. The paper must be stretched first, as explained on the preceding pages. Until you have practised the method it can be tricky to control the flow and spread of the ink, so begin with the larger areas of light washes and save the more detailed work done with the point of the brush until the later stages, when the paper has begun to dry or dried completely.

Ink and wash

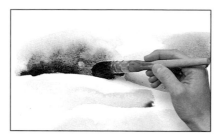

1 *Having laid some light washes of watered ink, the artist works into them before they have dried so that the darker ink spreads and diffuses softly.*

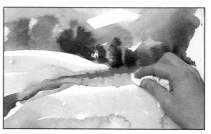

2 *Still working wet into wet, she uses a piece of kitchen paper to control the flow of the ink. In the foreground, the washes have formed blobs with irregular edges, an effect she likes and therefore makes no attempt to correct.*

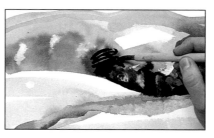

3 *The original ink washes on the trees have dried out to some extent, and the undiluted black ink now introduced hardly spreads at all. The artist is using a Chinese brush, which is ideal for this kind of drawing.*

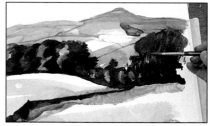

4 *For the final stages a crisp effect was needed, so the paper was left to dry before further work was done on the background, the foreground wall and now the trees.*

5 *(Right) The brush-and-wash method allows you to build up an impression of the landscape more rapidly than is possible with a pencil or pen. The finished picture also provides a good example of the way accidental effects can enhance a drawing or painting; the backruns in the foreground provide a touch of interest and echo the shapes of the trees.*

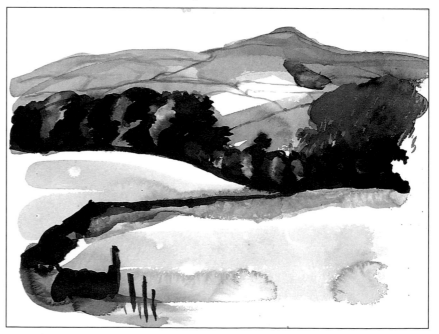

Brush and paint

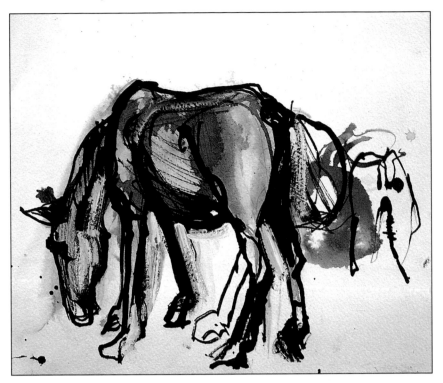

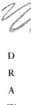

(Above and right) *In these studies, brush drawing has been taken a step further towards painting, with a combination of ink and watercolour used.*

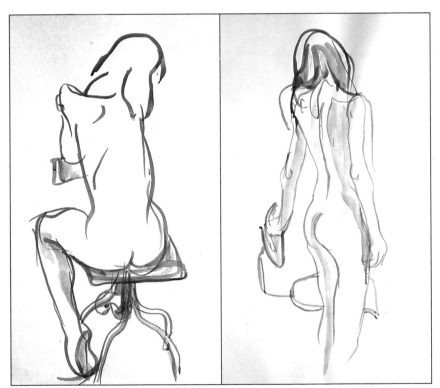

Brush and ink

Both these drawings were done in no more than ten minutes, with slightly diluted brown ink and a Chinese brush. The method is excellent for quick figure drawings and studies of movement.

THE BRUSH AS LINE

Another kind of brush drawing is that done with line alone, using the brush purely as a drawing tool. This also takes practice, and is slightly unnerving initially because you cannot correct errors; nevertheless it is an exciting method to try, and you may find that it releases some inhibitions and makes your drawing freer and less fussy. You can do almost anything with a brush, depending on the type you use, how you hold it and the amount of pressure you apply, so it is worth making some "doodles" to explore the possibilities. The Oriental artists and calligraphers, who have exploited the potential of brush drawing for centuries, have evolved many different hand positions; sometimes they work with the brush vertical and held loosely near the top of the handle rather than gripped firmly at the ferrule.

COLOUR DRAWING MATERIALS

Drawing with pencils, charcoal and pens provides valuable practice and can be highly satisfying too, but with the coloured drawing media you can really experiment and produce works which are as expressive and as polished as any painting. Today's artists are in the fortunate position of having a wide range of high-quality materials to choose from – the only problem being where to start.

COLOURED PENCILS

These make a good starting point for anyone launching into colour; they are easy to use, handling in the same way as the familiar graphite pencil, and you can start with a few colours and built up a more extensive collection gradually.

Like all colour media they are made from pigment held together with a binder. The quantity of binder used varies from one manufacturer to another, so you will find

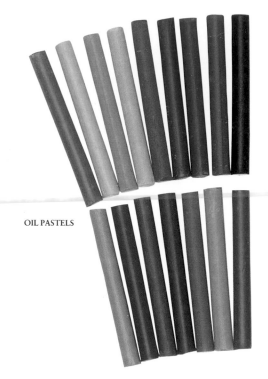

OIL PASTELS

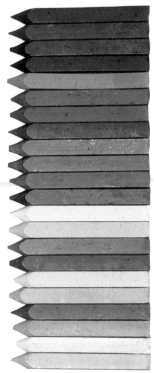

HARD PASTELS

differences in consistency between brands. Some pencils are soft, chalky and opaque, resembling pastels; some are slightly greasy, and others are hard and fairly transparent. You will only discover which ones you like by trying them out, which is one very good reason for starting with a small range.

SOFT PASTELS

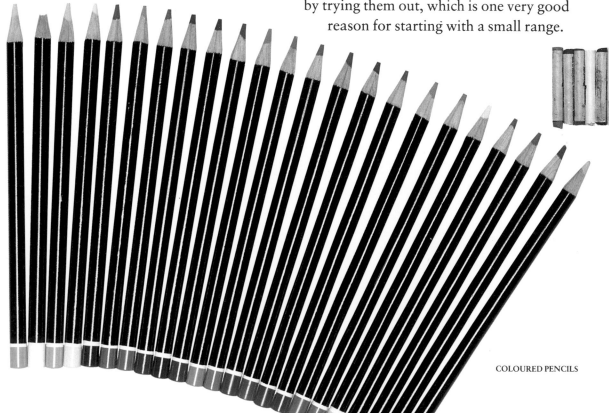

COLOURED PENCILS

Some manufacturers make water-soluble pencils as well, which are particularly useful because you can use them both wet and dry, spreading the colour in some parts of a drawing and using lines in others.

PASTELS

Pastels are made in soft and hard versions, with the former, sold in the form of cylindrical sticks, being favoured by "pastel painters". These are almost pure pigment, bound with a tiny amount of gum, and are consequently very crumbly. Hard pastels, made with a higher proportion of binder, come in square-sectioned sticks. They produce much crisper, clearer lines and do not smudge as easily. Pastel pencils are also good for linear effects – they are somewhere in between hard and soft pastels in their consistency. Spray fixative is necessary for any drawings in pastel.

Oil pastels have the great advantage of not requiring fixative, as the pigment is bound with waxes and oils. The variation in consistency from range to range is enormous, with some pastels being quite hard and others almost melting in your hand, but there are two basic categories: wax-oil pastels and non-wax ones, simply called oil pastels. The former have their devotees, but in general they are less malleable than standard oil pastels, which are a versatile and fluent drawing medium.

INKS AND MARKERS

Coloured drawing inks, like black inks, can be divided into two broad types: waterproof and water-soluble. They are made in a wide range of brilliant colours and can be mixed together to increase the range further. Some waterproof inks are bound with shellac, which means they can't be mixed successfully with water-based inks, but others are acrylic-based – they are known as liquid acrylics and they behave in use very much like water-soluble inks, except that they are impermeable when dry.

If you want your work to last, guard against the type of ink called "brilliant watercolour"; this is made not from pigment but from dyes, which can fade and discolour. The colours are temptingly vivid, but they are made for graphic reproduction work, where the discoloration of the original may not matter.

Some coloured felt-tipped pens are also prone to fading and should be checked carefully before buying. These pens are made either with broad wedge-shaped tips (these are sometimes called markers) or with fine tips, and the ink used in them can be water- or spirit-based. They are ideal for those who like a bold approach to drawing.

PAPERS

For coloured-pencil and oil-pastel work, and ink drawing, good-quality cartridge (drawing) paper can be used, though some artists who specialize in coloured pencil or oil pastel like to use a rougher texture and sometimes a pre-coloured paper. For chalk-pastel work, smooth paper is not usually suitable, as the pigment tends to fall off, so it is best to use either one of the papers made specially for pastel work – Ingres or Mi-Teintes paper – or watercolour paper. If you like the texture of the latter but prefer to work on coloured paper, you can tint it with a light wash of water-colour first.

MARKERS

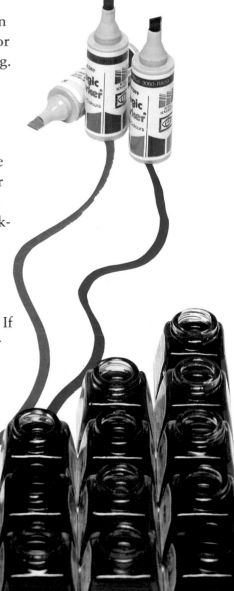

COLOURED INKS

COLOURED PENCIL

Although coloured pencils are becoming increasingly popular with fine artists, both for sketching and for finished works, at one time they were mainly associated with illustration work, and are still widely used for this purpose. In order to accommodate commercial demands, manufacturers produce coloured pencils in a wide range of hues and shades – some offer as many as two hundred. However, as colours can be mixed on the picture surface, it is not necessary to buy a complete range and, even if you did, you would still have to rely on mixing to some extent, particularly for dark colours, which can only be achieved by building up in layers.

COLOUR MIXING

Colours can be mixed in a number of different ways, the classic method being hatching and crosshatching, explained under pen and ink drawing. This method allows you to achieve subtle colour mixing effects as well as considerable depth of colour. Blues lightly hatched over yellow and then crosshatched in places with deeper blues will produce beautifully varied areas of green, while colour could be introduced into shadow areas by hatching and crosshatching over black with dark blues and purples.

While this is a good method for highly finished, detailed work, it is not a rapid process, added to which too many tight layers of hatching and crosshatching can make a drawing appear overworked and lacking in spontaneity. For a looser effect, tones can be built up simply by shading, the method you would naturally use with an ordinary graphite pencil. Colours can also be mixed in this way, with yellow shaded over red producing orange, and yellow over blue making green, for example.

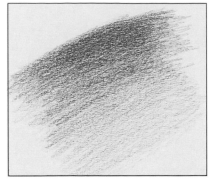

Colours and tones can be built up by careful shading.

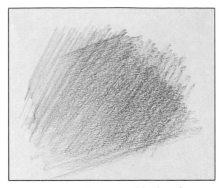

Colours are often mixed by hatching and cross-hatching.

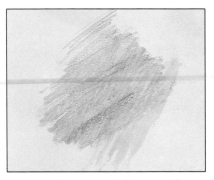

The tip of a water-soluble pencil has been dipped in water before laying the colour over the blue.

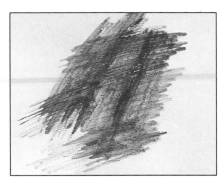

Both pencils have been dipped in water, and a wet brush taken over the whole area to produce this effect.

Burnishing

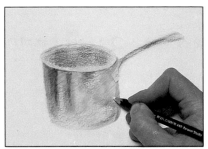

1 *The colours must be built up solidly in the part of the drawing to be burnished. Here a white pencil is used to burnish highlights.*

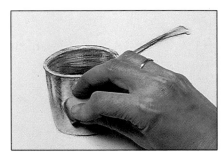

2 *An eraser removes a little of the pigment, but also pushes the remaining particles into one another, creating soft blends.*

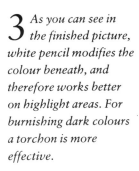

3 *As you can see in the finished picture, white pencil modifies the colour beneath, and therefore works better on highlight areas. For burnishing dark colours a torchon is more effective.*

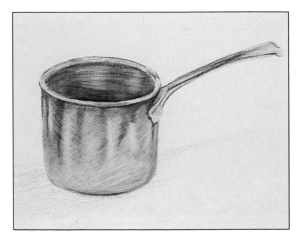

Impressed-line drawing

With water-soluble pencils the colour-mixing possibilities are increased; you can spread colour into a wash with water and a clean brush, overlay this with another colour, mix the second colour into the first with more water, and so on. However, don't overdo mixing wet washes of colours, as some of the coloured pencil pigments have a chalky quality and leave a muddy, colourless mess when mixed wet.

BURNISHING

This method can be used to increase the brilliance of colours in certain areas of a drawing, but it is not suitable for water-soluble pencils used wet. Having been built up thickly, the colours are then rubbed with a plastic eraser or torchon (a rolled paper stump sold for blending pastels). This action pushes the particles of pigment into one another so that no separate lines or marks are visible; the grain of the paper is flattened to produce a sheen.

IMPRESSING

If you draw with coloured pencil on a heavily textured paper, most of the pigment will be deposited on the top of the weave; impressing follows the same principle. "Blind" lines are pressed into the paper with a knitting needle or paintbrush handle and, when coloured pencil is applied on top, the lines show as white. The method is also known as white line drawing.

You can use impressed lines simply for variety in a drawing, but quite intricate pattern effects are possible too. If the white line is to play a major role in the drawing it is helpful to use tracing paper to place the lines accurately. Draw up your design, trace it – or draw it directly onto tracing paper – then lay the tracing on your drawing paper and go over the lines with a hard pencil.

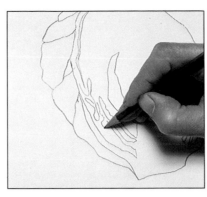

1 *If you are uncertain of the design you can work it out first on ordinary paper and then trace it, but in this case the artist draws directly onto the tracing paper.*

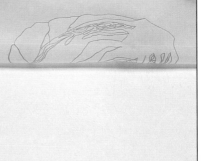

2 *She places the tracing paper over the working surface and, before starting the impressing, fixes it at the top with a piece of masking tape to prevent slippage.*

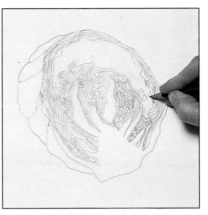

3 *She goes over all the lines with a hard pencil. You can use any pointed implement for this, but a pencil is the best choice for a complex design, as you can keep track of which lines you have drawn over.*

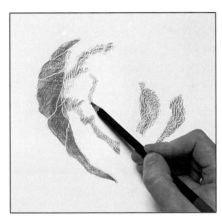

4 *The lines show up clearly through the coloured pencil, which is applied quite heavily. The working surface is smooth watercolour paper which, being thicker than cartridge (drawing) paper, produces more positive indentations.*

5 *With several reds and orange-reds shaded over one another, black is now used lightly to give greater depth of colour, contrasting with the white lines.*

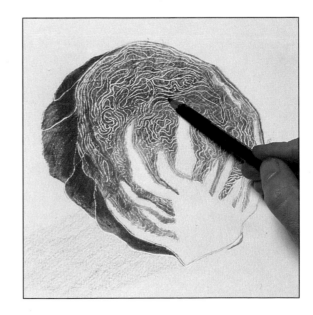

PASTEL TECHNIQUES

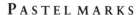

There is always argument about whether a work in pastel should be classified as a drawing or a painting, but this merely underlines the fact that there is no real boundary between the two. In general, a pastel with an obvious linear emphasis is considered to be a drawing while those in which colours are built up thickly in layering techniques and line plays a minor role, are clearly paintings, although not done with a brush.

PASTEL MARKS

In the context of drawing, it is the mark-making capacity of pastels rather than their ability to build up colours that is most important, and in this field they are supreme among the media. A coloured pencil can only produce lines and, although these can be thick, thin, heavy or light, there are few other possible permutations. Pastels, whether you use the hard or soft variety, have a far greater inherent range: they can be sharpened to a point to produce crisp, incisive marks, used blunt for softer lines, or broken into short lengths and used sideways to make strokes of colour.

Pastel pencils are less versatile in mark-making terms, handling very much like coloured pencils except that they are considerably softer. They are also softer than hard pastels and cannot produce the same fine lines that are possible with the edge of a square-sectioned hard pastel stick. However, they are pleasant to use, and excellent for relatively small-scale work. The colour can be partially spread with water and a clean brush to produce a wash effect and to soften lines where necessary.

OIL PASTELS

Oil pastels don't make very crisp lines either, but they are ideal for bold drawings

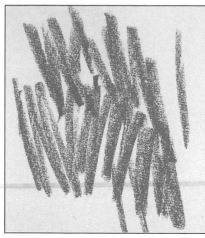

SOFT PASTEL

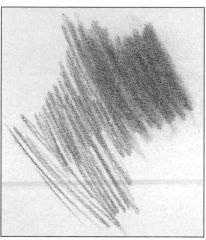

HARD PASTEL

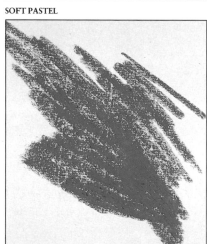

OIL PASTEL

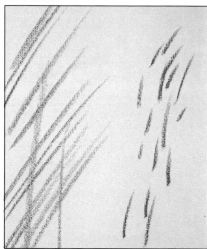

PASTEL PENCILS

and vivid, solid areas of colour. Some artists prefer them to soft pastels, as they are less crumbly, less fragile and do not require fixing. Furthermore, they allow you to make use of a technique called sgraffito, in which one layer of colour is scratched back to reveal another. A variety of effects can be achieved in this way, from fine lines made with a sharp implement to more subtle broken-colour effects, achieved by scraping back successive layers of colour with the edge of a knife.

PAPERS

The quality of the lines and marks you make with pastels, whichever kind you use,

Oil-pastel sgraffito

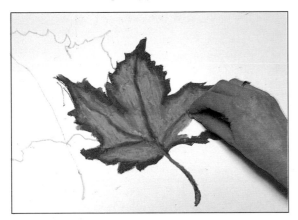

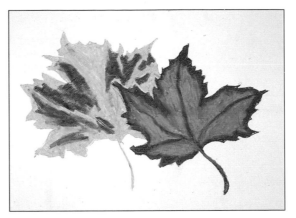

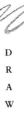

1 *Working on a smooth-surfaced watercolour paper, the artist lays the colours thickly, making sure that the oily pastel is pushed well into the paper.*

2 *Some areas of these first colours will be overlaid with darker ones, but selected parts will be either left uncovered or revealed by scratching, so the artist has chosen them with the finished effect in mind.*

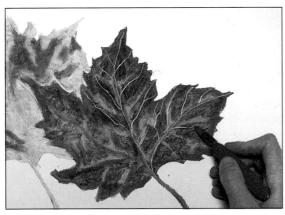

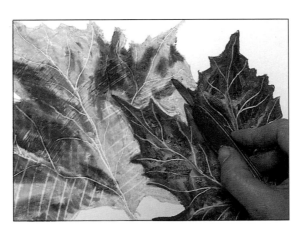

3 *With dark green now laid thickly on top of the yellow, the point of a knife is used to scratch fine lines. This has also removed a little of the original colour, but the lines are not white because the pigment has stained the paper.*

4 *The sgraffito effect has been built up all over the leaves, with varying pressure of the knife. Here it is used quite lightly.*

is considerably affected by the paper you work on. For a pastel painting, where you intend to build up colours thickly, it is usual to work on textured paper, as smooth paper does not grip the pigment sufficiently firmly. This reduces the solidity of the line, breaking up the stroke slightly so that some of the paper shows through. For purely line work, where you don't intend to lay one colour over another, you can use smoother paper, which gives a solid, unbroken line without the paper showing through. You might also try one of the special papers sold for pastel work – velour paper. This provides a line which is both solid and soft, with slightly fuzzy edges.

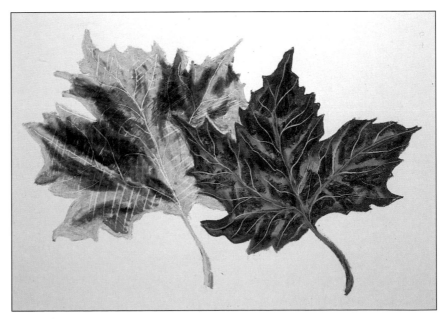

5 *Although you can scratch into light colours to reveal dark ones in exactly the same way, the technique is most effective when worked dark to light, as in this drawing.*

INKS & MARKERS

The idea of drawing with a brush can be taken a step further by using several different colours of drawing inks. These can be painted on straight from the bottle, mixed to produce a wide range of colours, or diluted with water (if you use water-based or acrylic-based inks) to form light washes of colour. In this way you can produce anything from a drawing made with several bold brushstrokes to something which closely resembles a painting in watercolour.

Coloured inks can be combined with black inks, applied either with a brush or a pen, or used in mixed-media techniques with other painting or drawing media such as acrylic paints, charcoal or oil pastels.

DRAWING WITH MARKERS

Markers and coloured felt-tipped pens are exciting to draw with, but because they are not capable of subtle effects, they are more suitable for sketches and quick impressions. Both markers (the chunky implements with broad wedge-shaped "nibs") and felt-tips are basically reservoir pens containing ink, which may be either spirit- or water-based. Water-based inks are better for sketching than spirit-based ones which tend to "bleed" into the paper so that some of the colour comes through onto the other side. The inks are transparent, so colours can be mixed on the paper surface by laying one over another; they can also be used in conjunction with drawing inks.

Markers on textured paper

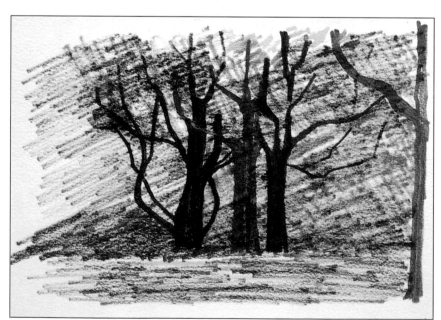

Used on smooth paper, markers create a solid, uncompromising line, but here the texture of the watercolour paper has broken up the strokes to produce a lighter effect.

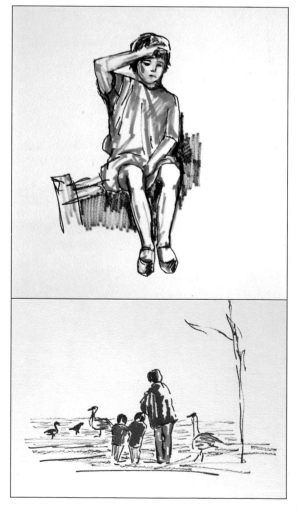

(Right, above and below) *Markers appeal to those who enjoy a bold approach, as they are not capable of subtle effects. They are, however, well suited to quick sketches such as these.*

Drawing with coloured inks

1 You can make a light pencil drawing as a guide for pen lines if you wish, but in this case the artist begins in inks straightaway.

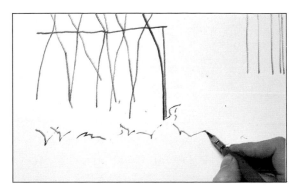

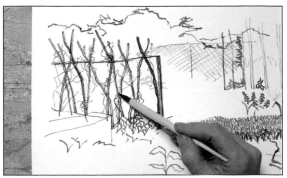

2 The purple flowers, and some lightly drawn red ones behind them, have provided a key for judging the other colours, and the artist now describes the shape of the patch of grass by making dark blue pen marks over green.

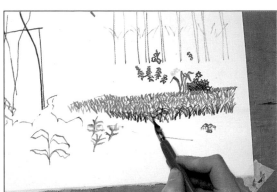

3 She is using a selection of different pens and has swapped the original broad-nibbed pen for a finer one in order to vary the quality of the lines.

4 The broad-nibbed pen is used again, as this area of the picture needs bold effects. Even with just one pen, the marks can be varied according to how it is held – notice how in the small plant on the left, the line changes from thick to thin.

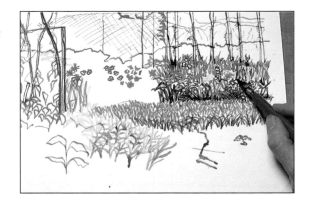

WAX RESIST

One of the best-known of the mixed-media drawing methods is wax resist, which is based on the incompatibility of oil and water. A drawing is made with wax crayons, wax oil pastels, an oil bar (oil paint in solid form) or an ordinary household candle, then water-based inks are laid on top; the wax subsequently repels the ink, creating a variety of fascinating effects.

5 The background and right-hand area of foreground have been left until last, as the artist wanted to establish the central area before deciding how to treat the other parts of the picture. The contrast between the fine lines used for the background and the bolder drawing of the foreground and middleground helps to create a sense of space as well as adding interest to the drawing.

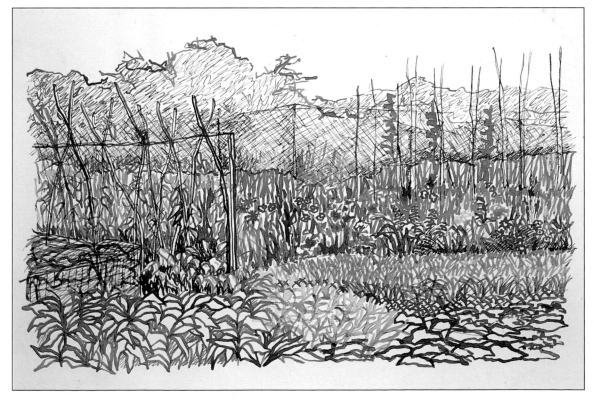

COMPARATIVE DEMONSTRATION

There is a wide range of colour drawing media on the market today, and you may need to experiment with several in order to discover which one suits your own style and pictorial interests which can be expensive. However, you can learn a lot by looking at and responding to other artists' work. For example, you may like the effects you see in coloured pencil drawings better than those achieved by pastel or oil pastel, in which case you would do well to follow this initial response. Here two artists demonstrate two

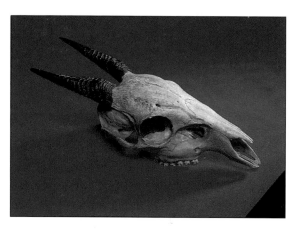

very different media in order to show how the medium affects your way of working. Elizabeth Moore creates subtle effects with coloured pencil, while Judy Martin has chosen oil pastel, a much bolder medium capable of strong, vivid colours.

Coloured pencil on cartridge (drawing) paper

1 *When there is any build-up of coloured pencil it cannot be erased, so the artist begins by working very lightly, making sure that the skull is correctly drawn before she continues.*

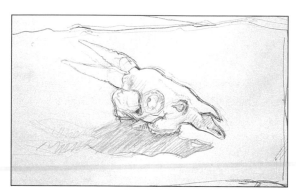

2 *Having established the overall colour of the skull, laying one colour over another in places, she now works on the shadow, which plays an important part in the composition of the drawing.*

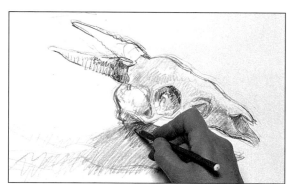

Oil pastel on coloured paper

1 *With a very light pencil drawing as a guide, the artist has begun with patches of white, dark browns and greys. Excited by the reflected colours on the skull, she works on these at an early stage.*

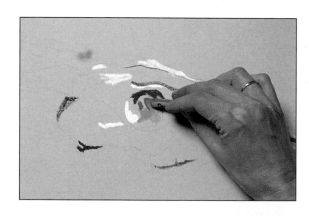

2 *The darkest and brightest areas of the picture have now been established – the vivid red background and one of the animal's horns. The red was particularly important because it would be difficult to assess the colours needed for the skull without some of this colour in place.*

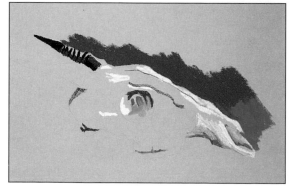

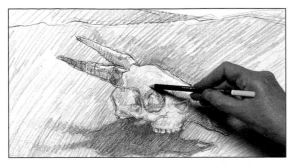

3 *In any line medium, whether pencil, coloured pencil or pastel, it is important to vary the marks you make, and here you can see a wide range, from long hatching lines on the table top to shorter, curving strokes describing the forms of the skull.*

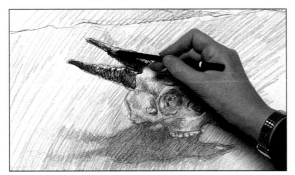

4 *Here again, over earlier light hatching, the artist has applied short jabs, squiggles and curving lines that follow the direction of the forms. Notice also the variety of colours describing the skull, and the subtle mixtures produced by laying one colour over another.*

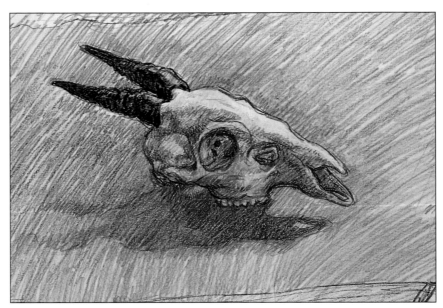

5 *If you compare the finished drawing with the oil-pastel one, you will see the extent to which the medium dictates the treatment of the subject. Because it is difficult to cover large areas with coloured pencil, the artist has only suggested the red paper, making the skull the most colourful part of the painting.*

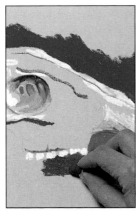

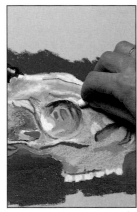

3 *As in the coloured pencil drawing, the shadow plays an important part in the picture. Although the arrangement is the same in both cases, the lighting was altered to produce a longer, more angular shadow.*

4 *The colours of the skull are now intensified. Because she is working on coloured paper, the artist uses white pastel for the highlights rather than "reserving" them as she would on white paper.*

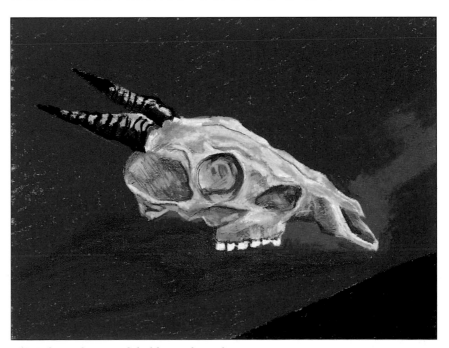

5 *Oil pastel is a much bolder medium than coloured pencil and, being soft, it covers large areas relatively quickly. These qualities have allowed the artist to exploit the dramatic red, black and white colour theme of the subject.*

MAKING ACCURATE DRAWINGS

D R A W I N G

Having looked at the different drawing media and seen the various effects they can achieve, the next step is to learn how to use them to make a drawing that describes your subject with the required degree of accuracy so that it looks 'real'. Accurate drawing should in no way be confused with detailed drawing – a few lines can provide a better likeness of a subject, whether it be a face, a figure or a landscape, than any amount of careful detail. It is largely a matter of getting the shape, the proportion and the relative scale of an object right, and this requires first and foremost careful observation and constant checking.

Learning to draw is like learning to write – the basic skills must be mastered before you can make them work for you. It is easy to be put off by early failures in drawing and to decide you simply haven't got "the gift", but you can minimize such failures by following some simple strategies, at least when you first start to draw.

DRAWING SIGHT SIZE
Most artists use some system of measuring when they draw, and this is easiest if you draw the size you see. The term "sight size" is self-explanatory, and many people draw in this way naturally. Others don't – they tend to try to draw as near as possible to life size, and have to force themselves to reduce their drawings.

You can check very easily what sight-size is by placing an object such as a mug on a table and holding up a sketchbook in front of it, in the position from which you might draw it. Then close one eye and make two marks on the paper, one for each side of the mug. If you are outdoors drawing a landscape or an urban scene you can make a series of these "placement marks" across the top of your paper. This can be done

Working sight-size

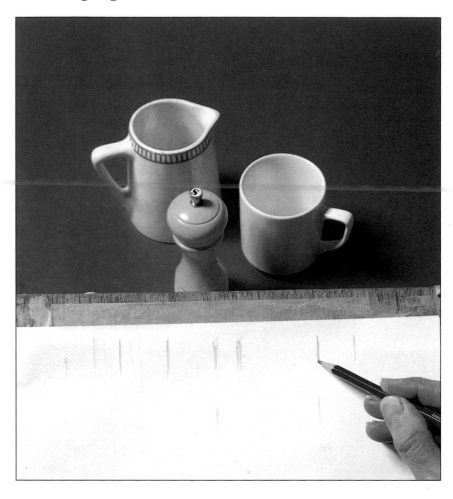

either by holding up a pencil at the same level as your drawing and moving your thumb up and down it, or by using a ruler and reading the measurements.

It may seem a mechanical way of drawing, but when accuracy is required it is very helpful. If you are making an under-drawing for a painting, for example, rather than just drawing for its own sake, accuracy is more important than expressive qualities, and you will avoid having to make corrections when you paint.

MEASURING BY COMPARISON
Drawing sight-size is easier than trying to scale objects up or down in your mind, but it doesn't always work because a sight-size

1 *With one eye closed, the artist begins by making a series of marks across the top of the paper so that he can establish the horizontal measurements. When drawing a small still-life group of this kind, you need to be quite close to the subject.*

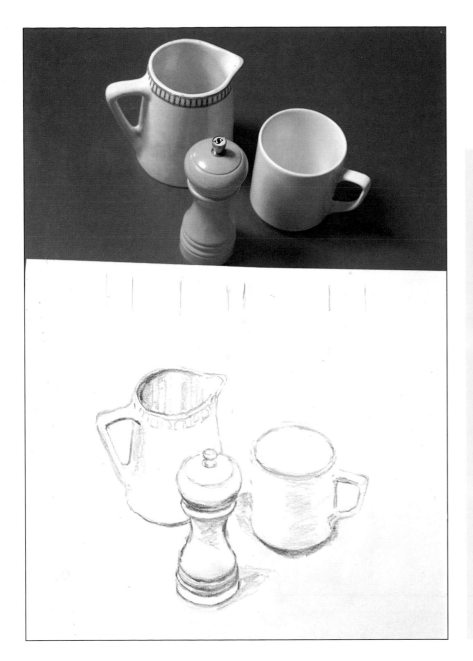

Making relative measurements

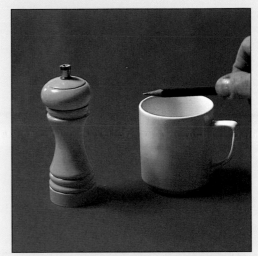

If you are not working sight-size, establish a "key" size, such as the width of the mug here, and relate the other objects to it. Make sure to hold the pencil at arm's length each time, as the measurements will not be accurate unless your hand is always exactly the same distance from the objects.

2 *With the first measurements marked in, the artist worked in the normal way, that is, with both eyes open. Only when he saw that something was not quite right in his drawing did he take further measurements, such as the height of the objects and the width of the ellipses.*

drawing can be very small. You can test this out in the same way as before, but this time hold the sketchbook close to the mug first and then about a metre away – the mug will become very small in relation to the paper. Drawing as small as this can be inhibiting – in a life class, for example, the model may be some distance away from you and, if you want to draw boldly in charcoal, sight-size will place unnecessary restrictions on your approach. In such cases you can still use systems of measuring, but you need to establish one "key" size and check everything else against this.

In a figure drawing the head is taken as the unit of measurement – there is more about human proportions later – but in any

drawing some major feature will help you work out relative sizes. In a drawing of an interior, for example, there may be a table or other piece of furniture which plays an important part in the composition. If you draw this in lightly first, you can then work out the scale of other features, such as the height and width of a window behind it, again by holding up a pencil. Try this out with the mug on the table again; first measure the height and then check the relative width. When not drawing sight-size, you must hold the pencil at arm's length and make sure you are always in the same position – the measurements will change as soon as you bend your arm or move forwards or backwards.

DRAWING SHAPES

Drawing involves, among other things, defining a shape by means of its outline, a fact which immediately establishes a kind of falsehood because no object is flat and there are no true outlines in nature. However, we still have to invent this outline because it gives us the shape.

MAKING AN OUTLINE DRAWING

It is not a bad idea to practise drawing shapes by setting up a simple group of still life objects – perhaps a mug, a plate and a bottle – and approaching them as two-dimensional shapes, drawing them in outline alone. This is not normally the way to make a good drawing because, although it may be accurate in terms of shape, there will be no suggestion of form and the objects will not look solid. However, it is a useful exercise as it does force you to look carefully and to analyse the shapes.

MAKING COMPARISONS

Drawing outlines becomes much easier when you begin to compare one shape against another and to check the relative sizes, as explained on the previous pages. Look, for example, at the way the shapes relate to one another. If you have placed them so that they overlap, how and at what point do they do this? Ask yourself how much larger, taller or wider one shape is than another, and in the case of a tall object such as a bottle, what the proportion of width to height is. A common fault is to treat each part of the drawing in isolation; it is no good drawing a perfectly shaped apple if it is too big for the plate on which it sits.

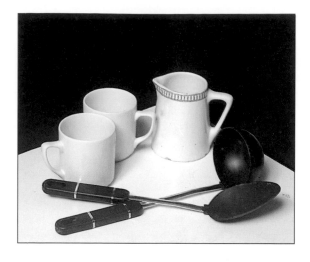

Improve your observational skills by setting up a group of household objects and drawing them first as positive and then as negative shapes.

Drawing outlines

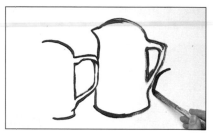

1 *This form of drawing is not easy and you will have to make corrections, so use a medium that allows this. The artist is drawing with a brush and acrylic paint, which she can correct by overpainting in white.*

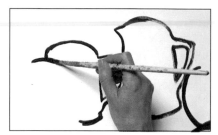

2 *Drawing an ellipse is difficult at the best of times, but even more so when you can only draw the top half. However, by looking carefully at the subject, the artist has managed well.*

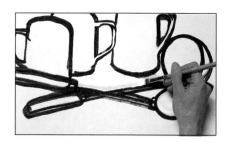

3 *(Right) The drawing of the spoon and ladle was not satisfactory, so white paint is now used to paint out the incorrect lines.*

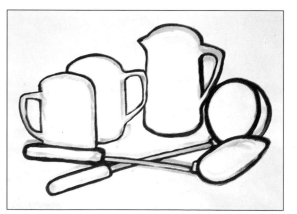

4 *The white paint does not completely cover the black, and a ghost line remains, which can be a helpful guide when correcting the drawing. If you erase completely, as you would in a pencil drawing, you are likely to repeat exactly the same mistake.*

NEGATIVE SHAPES

Another useful way to check the accuracy of a drawing is to look at the shapes between and behind the objects, known as negative shapes or negative space. If you are drawing a mug with a handle, forget about the handle itself and try to assess the shape of the piece of space between it and the edge of the mug. It can be helpful to draw these shapes before you turn to the positive ones; sometimes you may not have to draw the actual objects at all.

Drawing the negative shapes only is another exercise often set by art teachers and, although it seems slightly perverse, it helps you to sharpen your observational skills. It is also enjoyable, as it forces you to look at things in a completely different way and thus abandon any preconceptions. When your drawings become more ambitious, you can still use these systems of checking and comparing. Negative shapes are very useful in figure drawings, for example, when something has gone wrong but you are not sure what. In a standing pose with arms akimbo, you may have struggled so hard to describe the difficult forms of the limbs that you have failed to relate them properly to the body. You can often discover the mistake by checking the shapes of the spaces between arms and body.

Drawing negative shapes

1 *Again using a brush and acrylic paint, the artist is now drawing the still-life group "in negative", that is, she is painting only the shapes between the objects.*

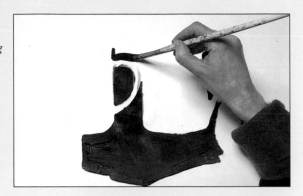

2 *Drawing in this way involves an initial effort of will, but it can simplify matters. Once you have trained yourself to look for the negative shapes, such as those made by the handles here, they can be easier to recognize than the objects themselves.*

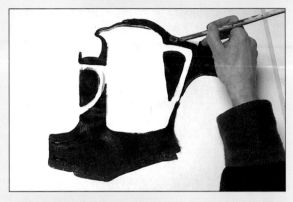

3 *As in the previous drawing, the artist uses white paint to make corrections. It is almost impossible to get everything right the first time in this kind of drawing.*

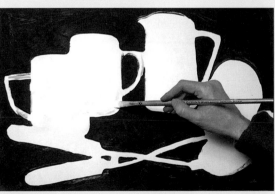

4 *Apart from helping you to observe carefully, drawing negative shapes has another function – it teaches you to consider the relationship of one shape to another, and thus to compose your work. This drawing, although not completely accurate, is lively and full of interest because of the balance between the light and dark shapes.*

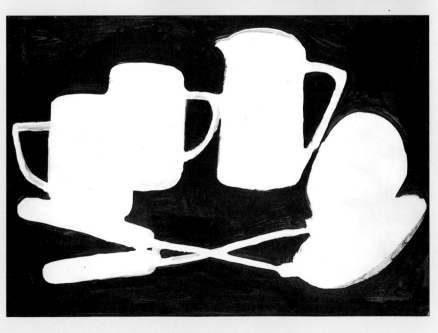

DRAWING FORM

So far we have looked at systems of measuring and checking to produce accurate outlines, shapes and proportions, but there is, of course, more to it than this. Drawing is a matter of creating illusions – you are portraying a three-dimensional world in two dimensions, and a good drawing must give a convincing impression of the three-dimensional form of an object as well as its outline.

JUDGING LIGHT AND DARK

Unfortunately no system of measuring can help you to describe the solidity of an object; here you must rely on direct observation, and this is less easy than it sounds. Form is described by the light that falls on an object, which creates light and

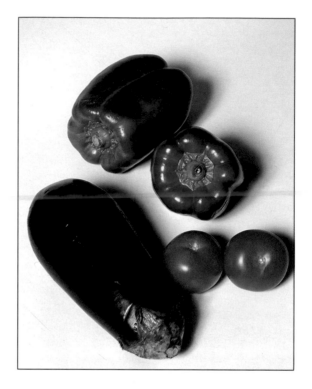

For this exercise you need a selection of rounded objects, preferably lit from the side to create well-defined areas of light and dark.

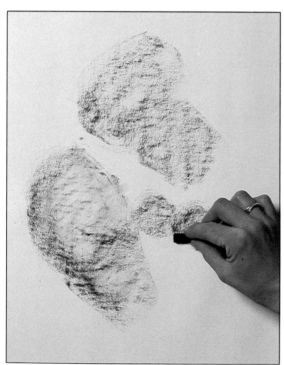

1 *Working entirely with the side of the charcoal stick, and thus avoiding the temptation to use line, the artist begins by blocking in the shapes of the various vegetables.*

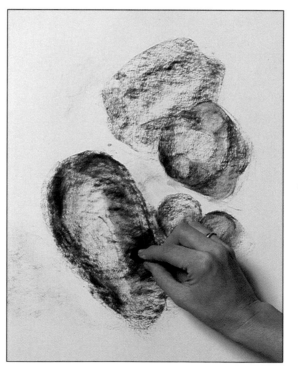

2 *Again using a short length of thick willow charcoal held on its side, she builds up the darker area of the aubergine (eggplant).*

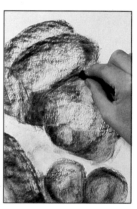

3 *The deep shadow between the two vegetables creates a dark line, so here the tip of the charcoal is used. Because charcoal is soft and smudgy, however, it does not give the impression of an outline.*

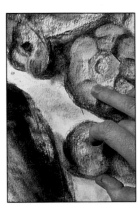

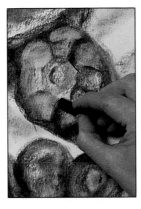

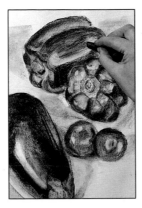

4 *A finger tip is used to rub off some of the charcoal, creating soft highlights.*

5 *The dimples at the top of the green pepper create rapid transitions of light to dark, so the shadows are deepened with the tip of the charcoal.*

6 *Because charcoal does not adhere well to smooth paper – the artist is working on cartridge (drawing) paper – dark areas often need to be re-established and emphasized towards the end of the drawing.*

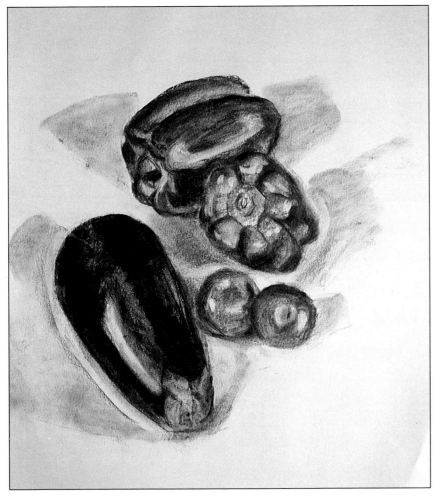

7 *Another danger with charcoal drawings is that the highlights can become lost through smudging, but this is easily remedied by the lifting-out technique. It has been used here for the two main highlights on the aubergine (eggplant) and the smaller ones on the top of the pepper.*

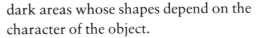

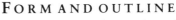

dark areas whose shapes depend on the character of the object.

If we lived in a black-and-white world it would be relatively easy to assess these differences in tone (the lightness or darkness of a colour), but more or less anything you choose to draw, whether it be a face or an apple on a plate, has colour. This confuses the issue, because our eyes register colour rather than tone, making it difficult to place the light and dark areas. It helps to half-close your eyes, which blurs the colour and cuts out much of the detail, allowing you to see more clearly in terms of tone.

FORM AND OUTLINE

Outline can be distinctly unhelpful when building up the impression of form, because a hard outline around a shape immediately makes it look flat. The outline of a round or cylindrical object, such as an apple or mug, delineates the boundaries of the form, that is, where it begins to turn away from you; if you put more emphasis on this than on the nearest part of the object, then the illusion of solidity is destroyed.

A good way to practise drawing form is to use tone from the beginning, avoiding outline altogether if you can, or drawing just a light outline for guidance. Try working with a broad medium such as charcoal used sideways, or try the lifting-out method. Of course you don't have to use charcoal – form can be described perfectly well in pencil or even pen and ink – but charcoal will help you to avoid a linear approach.

DRAWING WITH LINE

Having just explained how form is built up with tone, it may seem contradictory now to say that you can create an impression of three dimensions with line alone. It all depends on the quality of the line and how you vary it in your picture – whether it is solid and dark, light and delicate or soft and scarcely visible.

LOST AND FOUND EDGES

As we have seen, drawing a hard outline around something destroys its solidity because objects don't have hard outlines. Some of the edges may be relatively well defined because there is a shadow beneath, but others will be very soft and sometimes difficult to distinguish. These "lost-and-found" edges are an important concept in drawing, as they define volume. You can see the effect even on the simplest object, while more complex ones, such as flowers or the human face, are a mass of hard and soft edges caused by the different characters of the forms and the way they turn away from the light. By accurately observing these differences in line quality, you can produce a drawing which describes form without using any kind of shading. Although not easy to do, it is worth practising, as the results can be very expressive.

Observing edge qualities

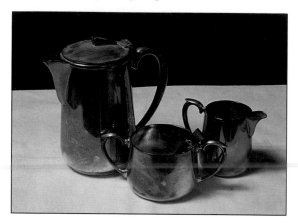

A combination of lost-and-found edges can be discerned in any object, depending on the lighting, the shapes and colour. If you can reproduce them accurately, you will be able to draw with line alone.

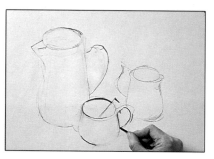

1 *Using medium willow charcoal, the artist begins with a light drawing, and is now strengthening the found edges on the sugar container.*

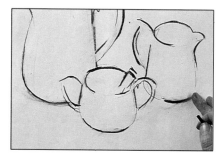

2 *She continues to clarify the edges, smudging the charcoal where softer lines are needed, such as in this shadow area. Edges at the bottoms of objects are often almost lost.*

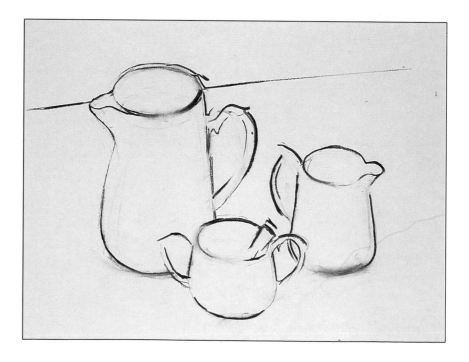

3 *(Right) Although there is no shading on the objects, the drawing gives a convincing impression of three-dimensional form, due partly to the lost-and-found edges and partly to the accurate drawing of the shapes, particularly the ellipses.*

Drawing with contours

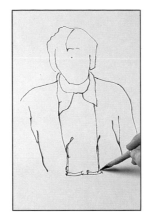

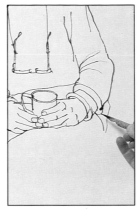

1 *To make this kind of drawing, it is helpful to restrict yourself to a medium which does not lend itself to shading. The artist is using a fine reed pen and black ink.*

2 *Having drawn in the basic outline of the model's head and upper body, she begins to add details such as the shirt collar and dangling spectacles.*

3 *Observing the lines made by the cuffs and the folds at the bent elbows has allowed the artist to describe the arms with no need to use shading.*

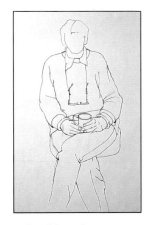

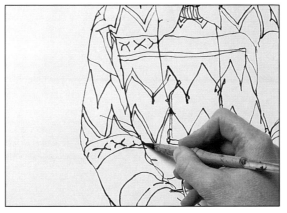

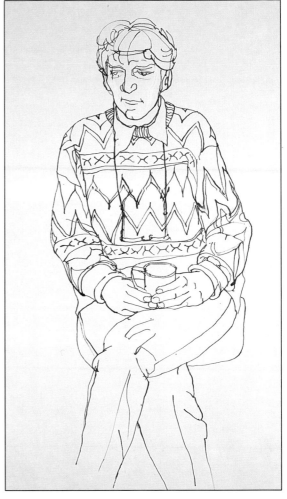

4 *Although not yet finished, the drawing is beginning to give a good impression of shape and form.*

5 *Pattern is a useful aid in the context of form, and here you can see how the behaviour of the pattern helps to explain the curves of the shoulders and the position of the arms.*

6 *The majority of drawings are a combination of line and tone, but it can be instructive to restrict yourself to line on occasion. Like all kinds of drawing exercises, this one gives you valuable practice in analysing your subject.*

CONTOURS

These are another way of using line to describe form. Contours are not the same as outlines; they are lines that follow the shape of the form. An obvious example would be a pattern curving around a piece of china; less obvious contours are provided by clothing – perhaps the sleeve of a shirt forming a series of folds and creases which define the form below, or the criss-cross of laces on a pair of shoes. Indeed, the clothed human figure provides a wealth of contours, from the line of a waistband indicating the curve of the body, to the cuff of a sleeve or a watch strap explaining the structure of the wrist. Not all objects, of course, provide such convenient clues to form – it would be difficult to describe an apple with contour lines – but, if they are there, try to use them in your picture, whether you draw with line alone or with line and tone together.

SKETCHING

There is no real difference between sketching and drawing, but the word sketch implies a quick study made either for pleasure or for reference, while a drawing can be a finished work with its own pictorial aims. There is, or can be, however, a difference between sketching for its own sake and making studies to be used as reference for another work, whether a finished drawing or a painting.

COLLECTING VISUAL MATERIAL

Artists often go through their sketchbooks to get ideas for compositions or simply to refresh their memories on some detail of a scene. The more you sketch, the more reference material you will have, and sketching also helps to polish up your observational skills. In some cases, however, sketches are made not randomly but to gather material for a composition, in which case it is necessary to consider the kind of visual notes required.

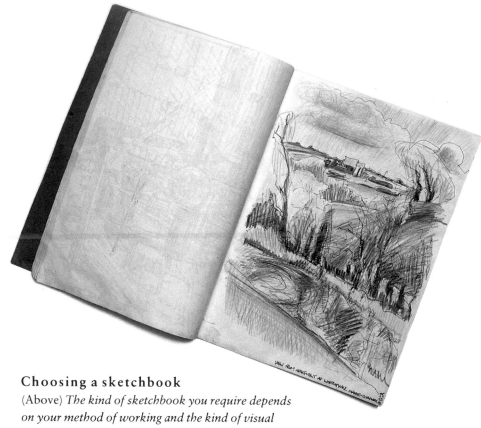

Choosing a sketchbook

(Above) *The kind of sketchbook you require depends on your method of working and the kind of visual notes you wish to make. Some artists have two or three in different sizes and formats. John Townend uses a large book for coloured-pencil drawings like this, and a smaller one for pen-and-ink drawings.*

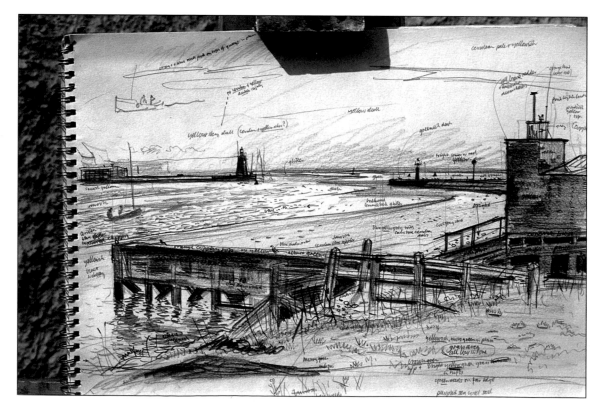

Sketching for painting

(Left) *This sketch by Stephen Crowther was made as the first stage in planning an oil painting, and the artist has made copious written notes to remind him of the colours. Using a large spiral-bound sketchbook enables him to remove the sheet and pin it up near his easel.*

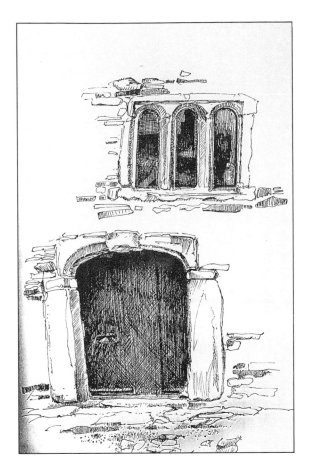

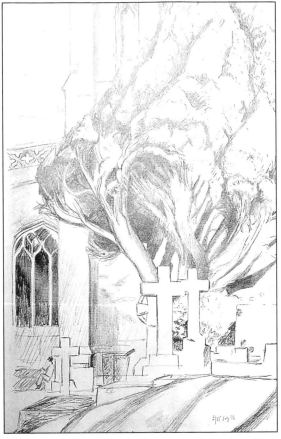

Choosing the medium

(Far left) *When you are out sketching it is wise to take a selection of different drawing media, as you may find that a particular subject is better suited to one than another. John Townend likes coloured pencil for landscapes, but prefers pen and ink for architectural subjects, where colour is less important than line.*

Collecting ideas

(Left) *David Cuthbert does not make sketches with a specific painting in mind, but he has several sketchbooks in which he notes down anything he sees, often taking photographs at the same time so that he has a store of possible ideas to hand.*

Making colour notes

(Below) *Gerry Baptist works mainly in acrylic, using vivid colours, and his watercolour sketches reflect his artistic preoccupations; a monochrome pencil sketch would therefore not provide the information that he needs for his paintings.*

Depending on the kind of work you are planning, you may need sketches in colour and tone as well as in line. Trying to make a painting from a line sketch in pencil or pen and ink is virtually impossible; you will have no idea what colour the sky was or which areas were dark and which ones light. It is wise to make a habit of including all the information possible on your sketches – if you don't have time to sketch in colour, make written notes about the colours. Do not simply write "blue" or "green", but try to analyse the colours; as long as you can understand the notes, this can be more valuable than sketching in colour, particularly if you intend to use one medium for the sketches and another for the painting. A sketch in coloured pencil, for example, would be very difficult to translate into watercolour or oil.

MATERIALS

For sketching you can use any drawing media with which you feel comfortable. Pencil is a good all-rounder, as it allows you to establish tone as well as line. Pen and ink

is useful for small sketches, but less so for tonal studies. Coloured pencils are tailor-made for colour sketches, and so are pastels and oil pastels, although neither of the latter is suitable for small-scale work. You can buy large sketching pads containing different colours of pastel paper, or you can clip pieces of paper to a drawing board.

Sketchbooks, usually containing cartridge (drawing) paper, can be bought in many shapes and sizes. Unless you like to work small, don't be tempted by a tiny address-book size, as you may find that it restricts and frustrates you.

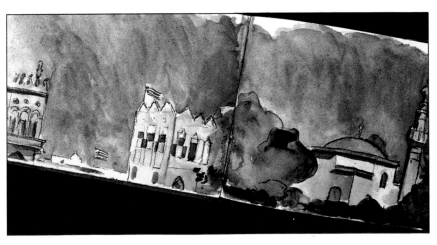

FIGURE DRAWING

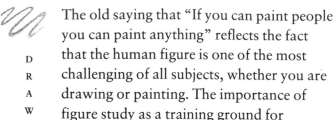

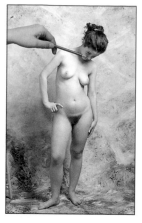

The old saying that "If you can paint people you can paint anything" reflects the fact that the human figure is one of the most challenging of all subjects, whether you are drawing or painting. The importance of figure study as a training ground for aspiring artists was recognized in the past, when drawing from life formed an important part of any art student's education. Nowadays there is less emphasis on it, at any rate in art schools, but amateurs flock to life classes, and many professionals return to them at stages during their careers to brush up their skills.

Joining a life class is not essential if you intend to restrict yourself to the clothed figure or to portrait studies; you can usually find someone who is willing to pose for you, or you can draw yourself in a mirror. However, for nude studies you must have a model as well as a decent-sized room in which to draw, so a class is the best answer; alternatively, you could share the cost of a model with friends or colleagues.

THE PROPORTIONS OF THE FIGURE

In the main, drawing is learned by practice, not from books, but books can provide some advice and point out things you may overlook when drawing. Figure drawings often go wrong because the proportions are not properly understood and, although human figures vary greatly, it is helpful to bear in mind some basic rules. These will prevent you from making heads and feet too small – a common error – and help you to analyse what is special about the body you are drawing.

Allowing for individual differences, the human body is approximately seven-and-a-half heads high. The mid-point of the body is slightly above the genital area, with one

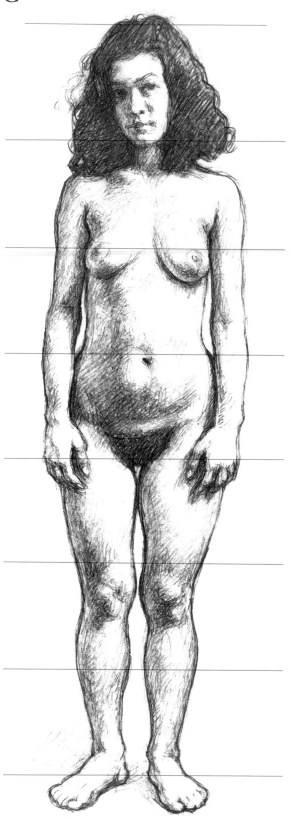

Proportions
Although the general rule is that the body is about seven-and-a-half heads high, it is essential to remember that there are variations; this model's head is relatively large. Observing these individual differences will give authenticity to your drawings.

Checking angles
In a pose like this it is important to represent accurately the slope of the shoulders and hips. Establish the precise angle by holding your pencil at arm's length and adjusting it until it coincides, then take it carefully down to the paper and mark in the line.

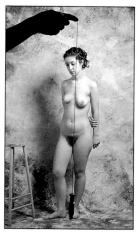

Checking balance
The centre of balance is vital in a standing pose, and you can check this either with a pencil or a plumbline, as shown here. This is a slightly laborious method, but is more accurate than holding up a pencil, where there is a danger of tilting it away from the vertical.

quarter point above the nipples and the other just below the knees. If arms are hanging loose by the side of the body, the wrists will be below the mid-point of the body, with the fingertips reaching to mid-thigh. The hand is about the same length as the face, from chin to forehead – try this out by covering your own face with your hand – and the length of the foot is approximately equal to the whole height of the head.

FORESHORTENING

In figure drawing, the head is always used as the unit of measurement, enabling you to make comparative measurements. Measuring systems become particularly important when the figure, or any parts of it, are foreshortened. Foreshortening is the perspective effect which causes things to appear larger the nearer they are; in a reclining figure, seen from the feet end, the feet will be large and the legs very short. It can be difficult to assess the effects of foreshortening accurately, partly because you know a leg is a certain length and find it hard to believe what you see, and partly because the forms themselves often change. In a seated figure seen from the front the thighs will be wide and short, because the flesh is pushed out by the body's weight.

Some degree of foreshortening is generally present in figure drawing and, because the effects created are often surprising, it is vital to take measurements. As you draw, hold your pencil out at arm's length to check the relative lengths and widths of limbs and body, returning to the head as the basic unit of measurement.

BALANCE AND WEIGHT

You can also use the outstretched pencil method to check angles, another common problem area. The angle of the shoulders or

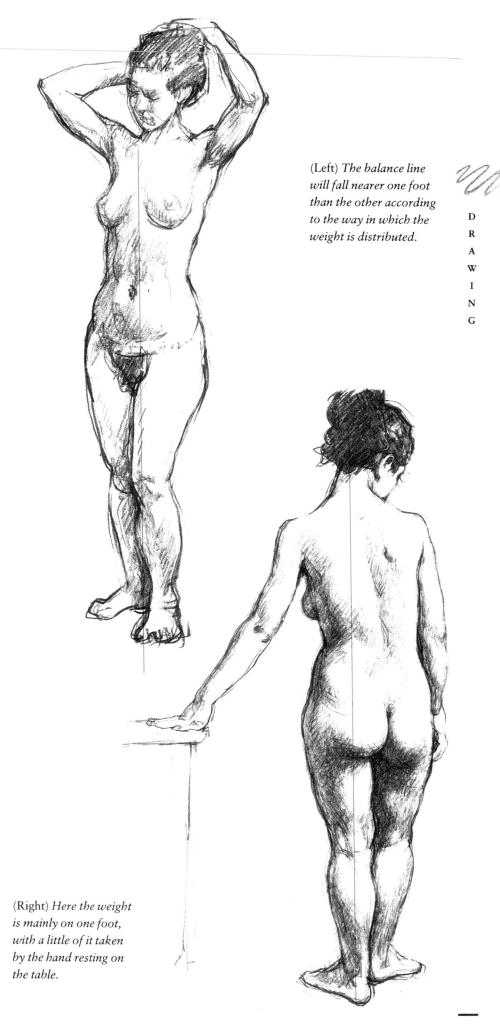

(Left) *The balance line will fall nearer one foot than the other according to the way in which the weight is distributed.*

(Right) *Here the weight is mainly on one foot, with a little of it taken by the hand resting on the table.*

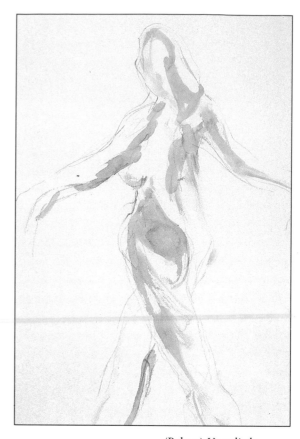

**Drawing
movement**
(Right) *To depict the
figure in motion, a
difficult but rewarding
subject, you need a
medium which actively
discourages detail. In
Arms Swing Hil Scott
has drawn with a brush
and diluted Chinese ink,
adding touches of
charcoal line. The
definition is minimal, yet
the drawing is an elegant
description of the fluid
lines of body and arms.*

(Left) *Here the weight is
divided between the arm
and the right leg, and the
shoulders and hips slope
in opposite directions.*

(Below) *Very little
weight is taken by the
feet in this stance, so
the balance line falls
some way outside them.*

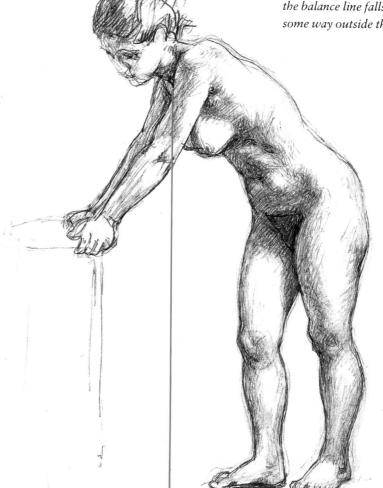

tilt of the hips often provides the key to the
pose. In a standing figure with the weight
on one leg, for example, the shoulders and
hips slope in opposite directions; whenever
one part of the body moves, another does so
in compensation, to maintain the balance.
Hold out your pencil and align it with the
shoulder or hip line and then, very carefully,
take the pencil down to the drawing and
mark in the angle as a guide line.

In a standing pose, "balance lines" can be
helpful; these give you the position of the
feet in relation to the body. It is vital that
this is correct, as your drawing will not look
convincing unless you convey an impression
of the way in which the body's weight is
distributed, and the feet, of course, are the
bearers of the weight.

Choosing the right medium

(Right) *Children are notoriously restless and usually have to be drawn very fast. It is thus wise to choose a medium which enables you to work quickly and broadly. Ted Gould has used brown Conté crayon for his lovely Mother and Child, suggesting both form and detail with a few deft touches.*

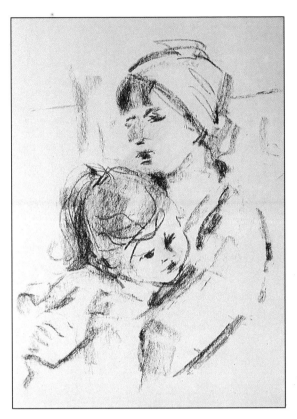

The standing figure

(Right) *As explained on the previous pages it is vital to analyse the pose and to understand how the weight is distributed and how the whole body is affected by any movement. In his two brush-and-wash drawings James Horton captures beautifully both the swing of the body, and also its three-dimensional quality of mass and weight.*

Balance lines are taken from the middle of the neck in a front or back view, and from the ear in a side view, down to the feet. If the model is standing with the weight evenly distributed, the balance line will be between the feet, but if most of the weight is on one leg it will be considerably nearer the weight-bearing foot. The most accurate way to provide yourself with these vertical references is to use a plumbline, which simply consists of a piece of string with a weight at one end.

The way in which the distribution of weight affects the body is less obvious in a seated pose, but it is equally important to identify it, or the drawing will look stiff and unnatural. Here again it is essential to check alignments, either with a pencil or a plumbline. You can either use the same system of balance lines or mark in a central

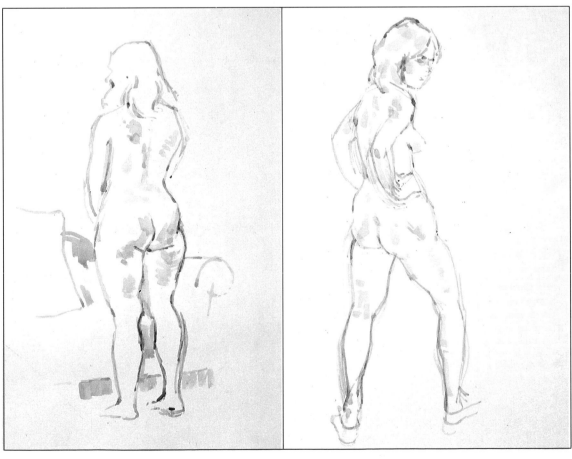

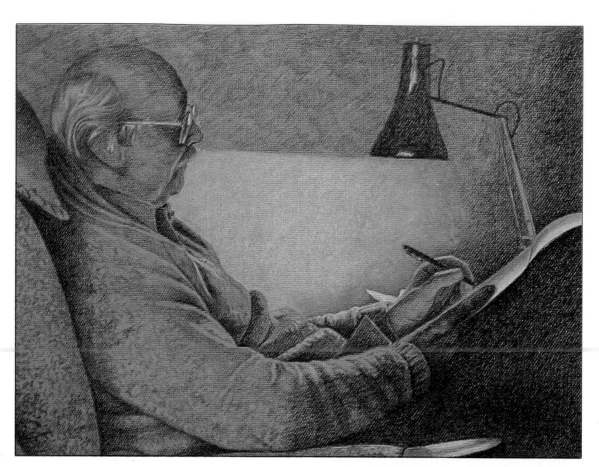

vertical line to which you can relate the position of the feet, head and various parts of the torso.

THE CLOTHED FIGURE

Drawing people with their clothes on is perhaps slightly easier than drawing the nude, if only because there is more opportunity to practise. You don't need a "proper" model because you can draw people anywhere as long as you restrict yourself to quick sketches. For more thorough and detailed studies, friends and family may oblige, indeed many people are flattered to be asked to pose.

Clothing can be helpful in defining the forms beneath it, providing a set of contour lines, but it can also disguise form and confuse the issue in a bewildering way. A thin garment, for example, reveals the body, while a heavy overcoat gives little idea as to the shapes beneath or to the way its wearer is sitting or standing. In such cases you must look for clues, such as the angle of a protruding wrist and hand, the bend of an elbow or the slope of the shoulders.

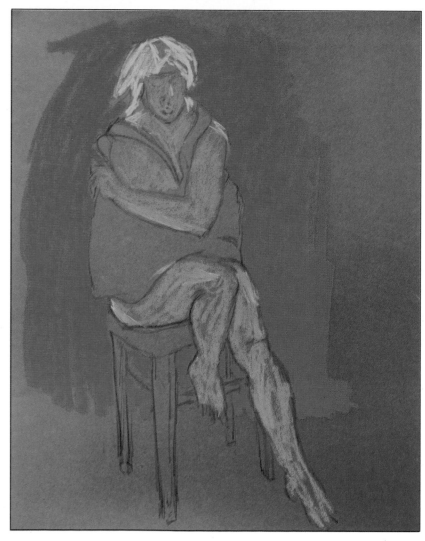

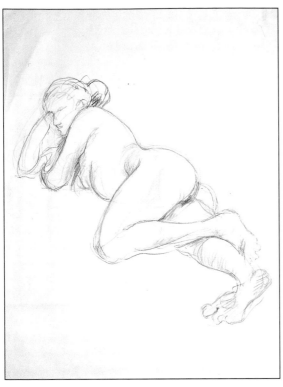

Whatever kind of garments your subject is wearing, try to visualize the body beneath. Analyse the pose just as you would in a nude study, taking measurements and checking alignments of head, shoulders, feet and so on, and perhaps drawing in some light guidelines to indicate key points, even if you can't see them. Clothing can be difficult to draw; it often forms complicated shapes of its own and you can become so involved with drawing folds, or the pattern on a fabric, that you fail to make sense of the figure itself.

Rounded forms

(Above) *This simple pencil drawing by Elisabeth Harden concentrates on the rounded nature of the female form. The relaxed pose of the model and raised left leg are depicted in a flowing outline, with no sharp angles used at all.*

Composing with shapes

(Opposite) *In his pastel drawing,* Elly, *David Cuthbert has made an exciting composition by reducing detail and concentrating on the interplay of shapes – the curves of the limbs counterpointing the more geometric shapes of the clothing and chair.*

Drawing light

(Right) *Forms are described by the way in which the light falls on them, so in life drawing or portraiture it helps to have a fairly strong source of illumination. In Gerry Baptist's simple but powerful charcoal drawing, the light comes from one side, slightly behind the model, making a lovely pale shape across the shoulders and down the hip and leg.*

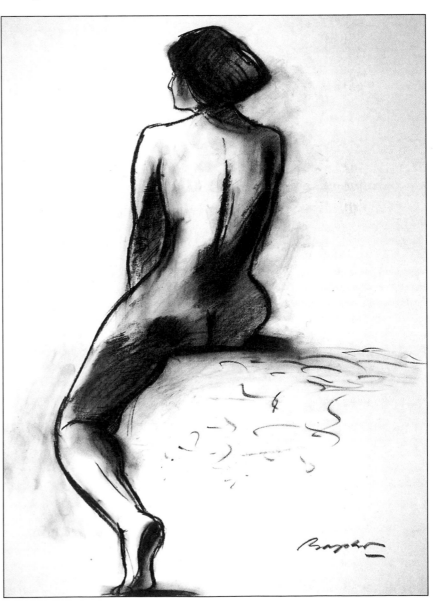

PASTEL DEMONSTRATION

James Horton is primarily a landscape painter, working mainly in oils, but for drawings he frequently uses pastels, which he finds particularly well suited to figure work. Pastel is both a drawing and a painting medium, depending on how it is used, and he exploits its linear qualities, building up colours with light layers of hatching and crosshatching so that each line remains distinct. He avoids the techniques closely associated with pastel painting, such as side strokes, blending and overlaying layers of thick, solid colour.

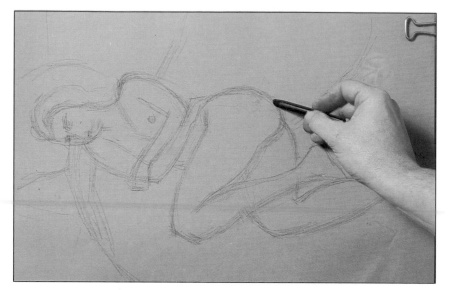

1 *Because pastels cannot easily be erased it is important to begin with an accurate drawing. This is made with a stick of compressed charcoal; pencil should not be used for pastel work, as the slight greasiness of the graphite repels the pastel colour.*

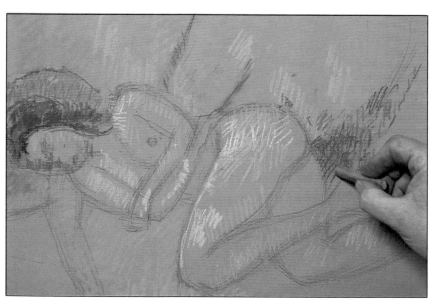

2 *The artist begins by placing small areas of colour all over the picture, relating the rich background colours to the subtler flesh tints. The coloured paper (Ingres) provides a middle tone, making it easier to work up to the highlights and down to the darks.*

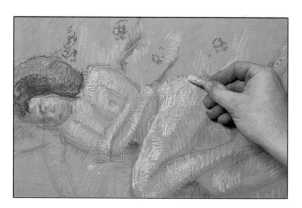

3 *This stage clearly illustrates his method of hatching and cross-hatching. He holds the pastel stick lightly and takes care to vary the lines so that they do not all go in the same direction.*

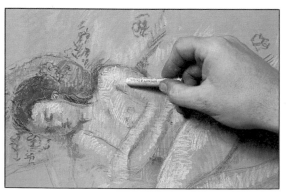

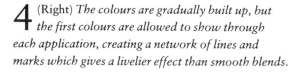

4 *(Right) The colours are gradually built up, but the first colours are allowed to show through each application, creating a network of lines and marks which gives a livelier effect than smooth blends.*

5 *At this stage much of the paper is still uncovered, but it does not need to be covered completely, as the light greenish-brown is very close to the colour of the shadows on the flesh. Choosing the right paper colour is an important aspect of pastel work.*

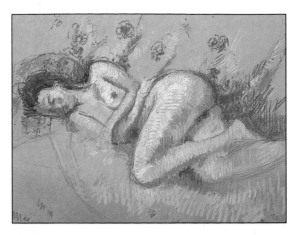

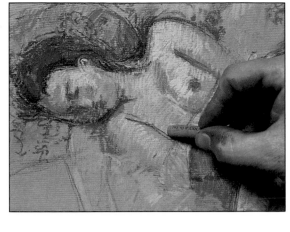

6 *The compressed charcoal is used again to darken and define areas of the hair and to sharpen up the drawing. Charcoal mixes well with pastel, and can be a better choice than black pastel, which makes solid and sometimes over-assertive black lines.*

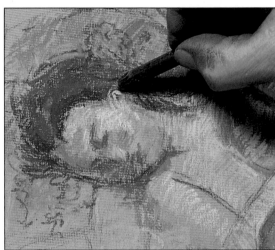

7 *(Above) The process of building up the darker colours and defining details continues, with brown pastel now used lightly to draw the side of the arm. On the shoulder, some of the original charcoal drawing is still visible, and has been strengthened by curving lines of red-brown pastel behind it.*

8 *(Below) The artist has not attempted to treat the background or foreground in detail, concentrating instead on the rich, golden colours of the body. This vignetting method, in which the focal point of the picture is emphasized by allowing the surrounding colours to merge gently into the toned paper, is a traditional pastel-drawing technique.*

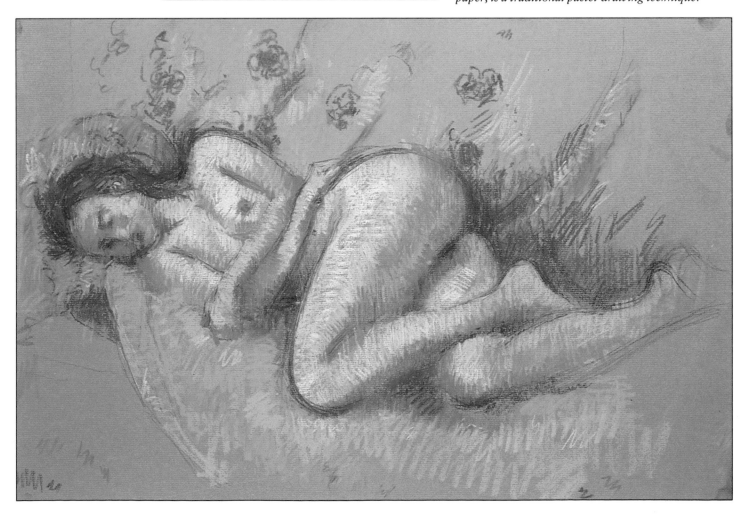

Focus
ANIMALS

Drawing animals can be rewarding and frustrating in equal measure. Whether they are wild creatures, farm animals or household pets, animals make wonderful subjects – it is enjoyable simply watching them – but unfortunately they are not the most co-operative of models. Even cats, which generally sleep for long periods, have a tendency to wake up and walk away as soon as you reach for your sketchbook. However, many artists have portrayed animals successfully, purely because they were fascinated by them, and this should be your sole criterion in choosing your subject matter.

OBSERVATION AND SKETCHING
As with any branch of drawing, the secret lies in careful observation of detail, the determination not to be put off by failures and, most important of all in this context, the ability to tailor your methods to your subject. You will certainly not be able to produce the kind of finished drawing you might achieve with a figure or an architectural subject, but you can make quick sketches, and a good sketch often says more than any amount of detail and polish.

You may find it difficult at first, because it does require some practice to be able to grasp the essentials of a subject and get them down on paper in a few minutes, or maybe just a few seconds. However, you will find that even your first, perhaps not very successful sketches will have sharpened your observational skills, and the next sketches will be better for this reason. Sketching is a knack, and it really does become easier the more you do it. Use a medium you know you can control well and one that enables you to work quickly in both line and tone – soft pencil, Conté crayon or pastel are all suitable.

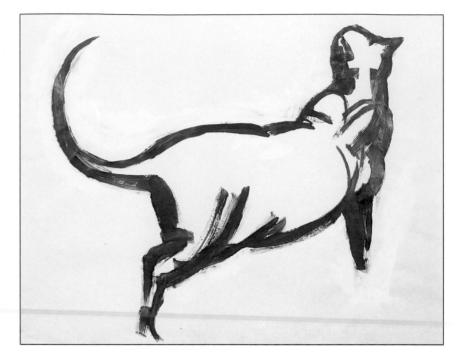

Rhythm and movement
(Above) _In an animal drawing, as in a figure study, it is important to convey the living quality of the creature and the way it moves, so choose a medium which allows you to work rapidly and freely. Judy Martin's_ Cat Study _is a large-scale drawing: she likes to work "from the elbow", and has drawn directly with a brush and acrylic paint. The diagonal placing of the animal on the paper, together with the sweeping curve of the tail, give a strong sense of movement._

Drawing texture
Texture, whether the rough, shaggy hair of a dog, the soft fur of a cat or the lustrous plumage of a bird, is one of the most attractive features of animal subjects, but you cannot concentrate on these qualities when you are trying to draw animals in motion so you will often have to work from photographs or museum specimens. In his pencil drawing Dead Bird _Robert Maxwell Wood has taken advantage of the mortality of all creatures, to provide himself with an excellent subject for close study._

D R A W I N G

52

Shape and pattern
(Right) *This pencil drawing is a preliminary design for a print, a medium in which three-dimensional form is less important than the arrangement of shapes. What first attracted Elisabeth Harden to the subject was the shapes of the animals' markings, which she has stressed with firm outlines and shading.*

Multiple drawings
(Far right) *Animals tend to repeat their movements, and another approach is to do several drawings on one page and work on them at the same time, as Vicky Lowe has done in her brush-and-wash studies of rabbits. Not only does this help in practical terms, as you can move on to another drawing as soon as the creature moves, but it also creates an impression similar to an animated cartoon.*

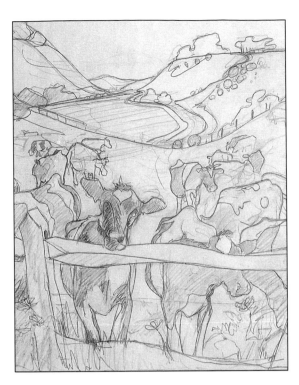

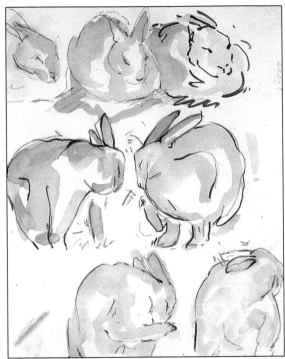

REPEATED MOVEMENTS
There is an element of memory involved in drawing anything in motion, particularly if the movement is rapid, because our eyes simply can't keep up with it. There is no one split second in which you can say "Ah, that's what the legs are doing." It is interesting to note that even the great 18th-century British artist George Stubbs, who specialized in horses, was unable to portray them convincingly in motion. It was not until the era of photography that the sequence of movements made by a

galloping horse was fully understood. Now that we know how a horse moves, it is much easier to appreciate the repetitive nature of most animals' movements. Look for these repeated movements when you are sketching, making several small sketches on the same page so that you have a complete visual record of all the different positions of the legs and body.

PHOTOGRAPHIC REFERENCE
The advent of photographs was invaluable to the 19th-century painters in correcting misconceptions about movement, and they still play an important part in providing reference for drawings and paintings. If you want to draw wild animals – which seldom even appear to order, let alone stay still – photographs are generally the only option available for reference.

Keeping up with movement
(Left) *Even when quietly grazing, animals will shift their weight from one leg to another and make other small changes in their position. Do not try to change your drawing each time; instead simply draw one line over another, as Karen Raney has done in her coloured-ink drawing of* French Horses. *As can be seen, she has begun with light lines and washes, and has delayed finalizing the positions of limbs and feet with more positive colours until the later stages.*

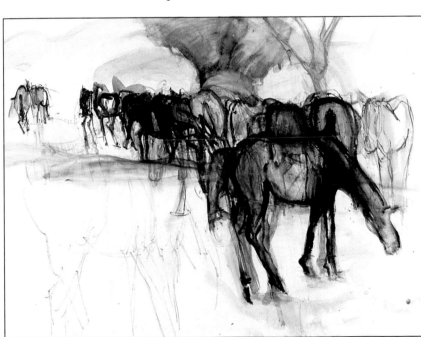

COLOURED-PENCIL DEMONSTRATION

Judy Martin is not a professional animal artist; indeed she sees herself primarily as an abstract painter. She has, however, always been fascinated by animals, and at one point in her career drew and painted little else. From time to time she returns to such subjects with enjoyment, working mainly from photographs but always interpreting photographic reference in order to create her own compositions and colours. Here a photograph is used as the basis for the cat, but the background and foreground are imaginary.

1 *Here the artist is working with water-soluble pencils on watercolour paper. She begins by laying some light lines and then washes over them. This releases some of the colour and softens the pencil marks without disturbing them.*

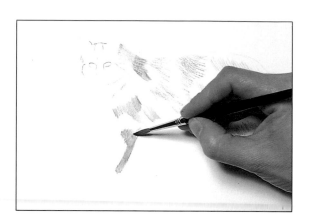

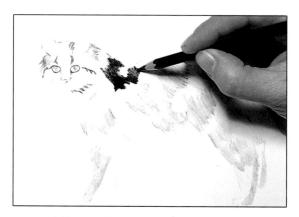

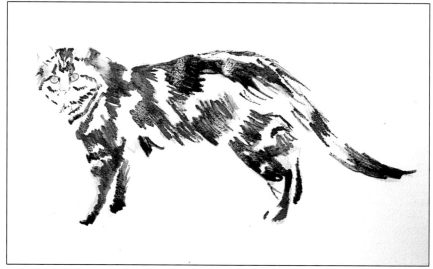

2 *A different effect is created by dipping the pencil into water before applying it. As you can see, this produces a more solid area of colour.*

3 *With dry coloured pencils, dark colours have to be deepened gradually, but water-soluble pencils make it easier to establish the dark tones at an early stage.*

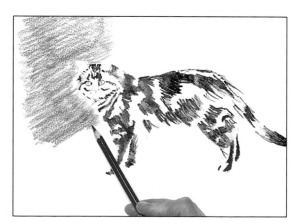

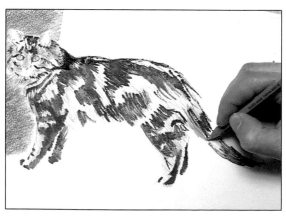

4 *With the dark and light tones of the cat established, the artist can now consider the background. A solid area of colour on the left is needed to provide a balance for the animal, plus a contrast of textures, so here she uses the pencil dry.*

5 *Warm reddish browns have been introduced with a dry pencil to suggest the texture of the fur. A wet grey pencil creates a soft effect on the tail.*

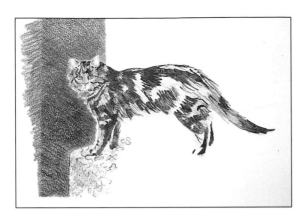

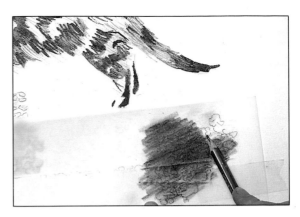

7 (Right) *Building up a complex pattern is a slow process and it is easy to make mistakes; to guard against this, a tracing is made from the completed area and the lines transferred to the working surface.*

6 (Above) *The dark background has been completed, with black cross-hatched over the blue, and a patterned cloth (which was not in the photograph) has been invented to create some interest in the foreground. As it is difficult to work without visual reference, a piece of fabric from the artist's collection of still-life draperies provided the basis for the pattern.*

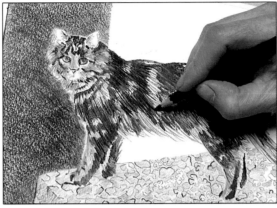

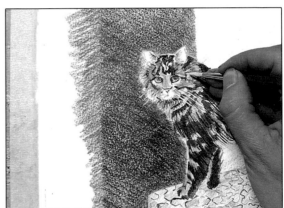

8 *With the background and patterned cloth finished, the artist returns to the focal point of the picture, and builds up detail and texture with a combination of wet-and-dry applications of pencil.*

9 *Finally, she uses white gouache paint and a small brush to touch in the whiskers. Coloured pencils are less opaque than either pastels or gouache paints, so clear whites cannot be produced by drawing over dark colours with white pencil.*

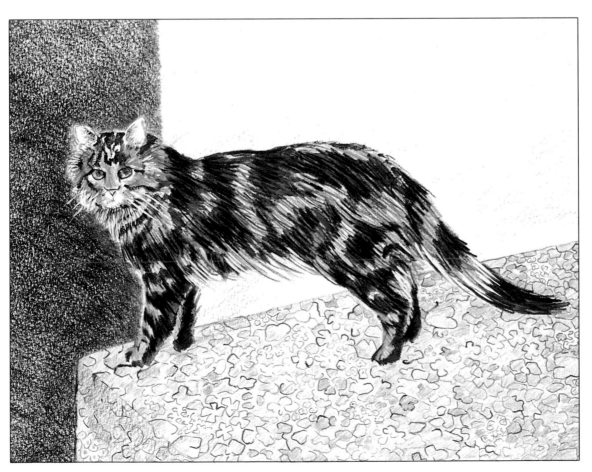

10 *In any finished drawing, the composition is as important as the representation of the subject; here careful planning has balanced the elongated shape of the cat's body with the patterned cloth and the dark rectangle of the background.*

BUILDINGS

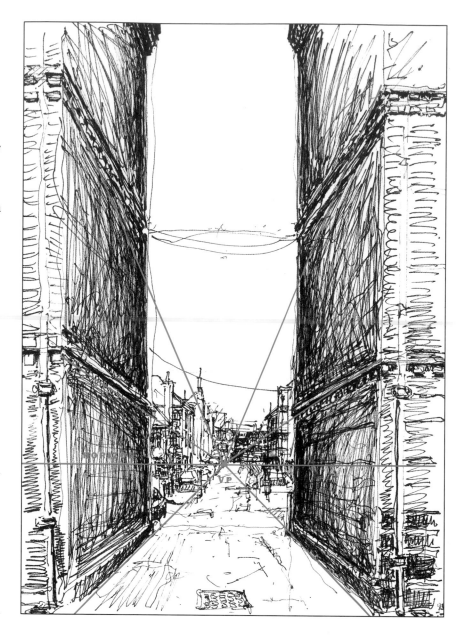

The man-made environment of cities, towns and villages provides a wealth of varied and exciting drawing subjects, whether you are interested in architectural styles or simply in atmosphere. It is sometimes thought that drawing buildings is a special skill, but, although detailed "architectural renderings" are specialized and have a particular purpose, buildings and townscapes present no more of a problem than any other subject, and are almost certainly easier than drawing the nude figure. What puts many people off is the word "perspective" – most of us know that linear perspective is based on mathematics and, for those of us who failed to grasp geometry at school, that is quite enough to cause alarm and despondency.

CONVERGING PARALLELS
It is true that the laws of perspective were arrived at originally through mathematics, but it is not true that they cannot be understood by non-mathematical people. The basic rules are really very simple, and they always bear out the evidence of your own eyes. Most people must at some time have walked or driven down a straight road and noticed how the two sides converge in the distance. This apparent meeting of receding parallel lines is one of the many tricks the eye plays with reality – the lines don't really meet, but in visual terms they do, and drawing is concerned with what we see. Without perspective it would be impossible to create the illusion of our three-dimensional surroundings on a flat piece of paper.

As parallel lines appear to come closer and closer together until they meet, it follows that things get smaller the further away they are. Imagine a row of identical buildings along the road. If you were to

draw one line through the top of the roofs and another below the doors, they would be receding parallel lines too, and would meet at the same place as those for the sides of the road, with the houses becoming smaller and smaller. Again, the effect of this law of diminishing size is something that everyone must have observed.

VANISHING POINTS
The place where the parallel lines meet is called the vanishing point, for obvious reasons, and it is located on an imaginary line called the horizon. This is the most important fact of all because, although the line is imaginary, it isn't arbitrary – it is your own eye level. This is why perspective changes as soon as you move your own

Central vanishing point
(Above) *The drawing has been done from a central position, so the vanishing point is also in the centre, with the receding parallel lines sloping down to the horizon line, which is at the level of the artist's eye. In fact the receding lines at the top of the drawing are not entirely correct – they should slope more steeply – but drawings can often be the better for small inaccuracies in the perspective.*

Moving position

(Right) *The artist has now moved to the left in order to see more of the right-hand wall, and the vanishing point has also changed position. The horizon, however, remains constant, as this drawing has been done from the same level as the first one.*

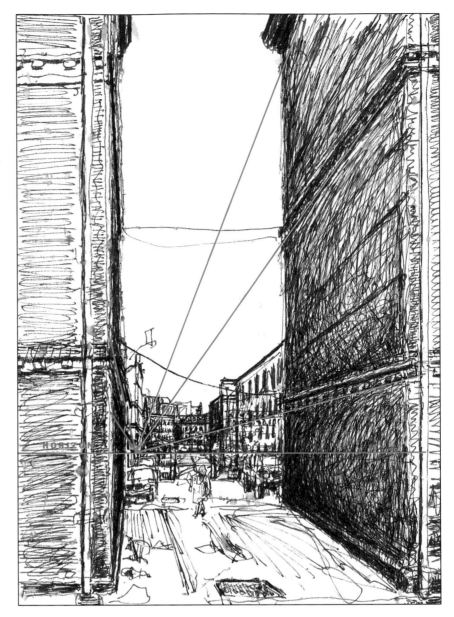

viewpoint, even from a sitting to a standing position. You have changed the horizon, the vanishing point and the direction of the parallel lines.

There is, of course, one further complication: there are often two or more different vanishing points, depending on your angle of viewing. If you are drawing a house from an angle, both planes will be receding from you, so lines drawn through the tops and bottoms of each would meet at their own separate vanishing points. In an old town or village, houses may be set at odd angles to each other, resulting in many different vanishing points.

PERSPECTIVE BY EYE

In such cases you cannot possibly establish the exact position of each vanishing point, but it is important to mark in the horizon line and, if possible, the vanishing point for one key building of the scene before you. You can work out the other receding lines by holding up a pencil or ruler and tilting it

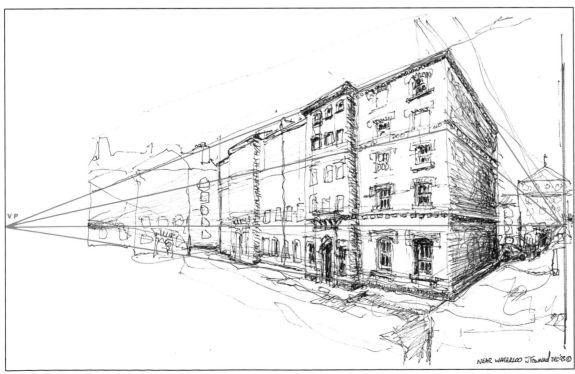

NEAR WATERLOO JTOWNEND DEC '93 ©

Two vanishing points

(Left) *The majority of architectural subjects have at least two different vanishing points, depending on how many planes there are and the angle from which they are viewed. Here there are two, with the converging parallels sloping more sharply down to the horizon line on the right. All three drawings, by John Townend, are in pen and ink.*

Continued ▷

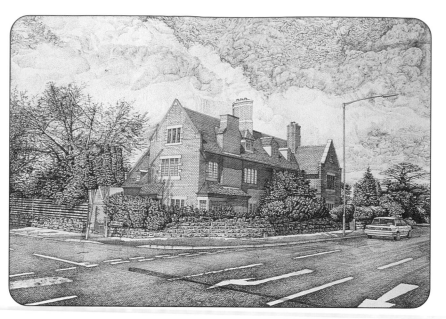

Perspective and proportion
(Left) *In Paul Bartlett's pen-and-ink drawing, a study made for a painting, the perspective is impressively accurate, as is the observation of the building's proportions. Notice the care taken over the number of bars in each window and the exact size of each brick and roof tile.*

Shapes and colours
(Below) *Town scenes, which present a variety of different elements, provide an opportunity to explore contrasts of shape, surface texture and colour. In his sketchbook study in coloured pencil, David Cuthbert's interest has been primarily in the lively patterns made by the buildings, street furniture, flags and shadows.*

Interiors
(Below) *The inside of a building is as interesting and rewarding to draw as the exterior, and you have the additional bonus of being protected both from the weather and inquisitive eyes. In his pen-and-ink drawing* The Church Organ Before Renovation *John Townend has made an exciting composition based mainly on the interplay of curves and diagonal lines.*

until it coincides with the angles of the roof, window tops or other features, as explained under figure drawing.

You do not have to get all the vanishing points exactly right – indeed this will be impossible, as many of them may be outside the picture area – but do make checks from time to time if you see something that doesn't look right. If you misjudge one angle and try to relate all the others to it the drawing will become distorted. And if you are bad at drawing straight lines don't be afraid to use a ruler, at least at the start of a drawing. Vertical lines really do have to be vertical in architectural subjects.

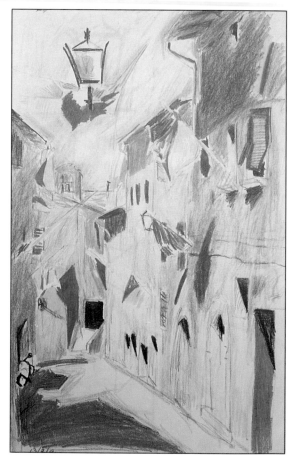

SCALE AND PROPORTION
Proportion is every bit as important as perspective – perhaps even more so. While it is correct (or reasonably correct) perspective which makes a drawing look realistic and the building not about to fall over, it is well-observed proportion which conveys character. You would not expect to draw a portrait without paying attention to the size of your sitter's eyes in relation to his

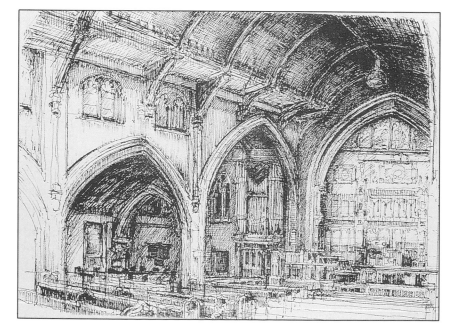

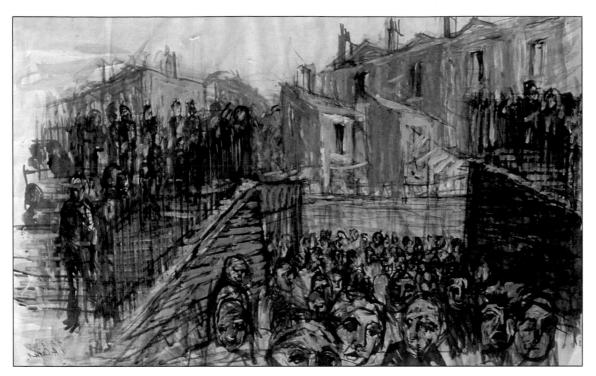

**Buildings as a
setting**
(Left) *In Gerald Cains's
mixed-media drawing*
Open End, Ashton Gate
*(in acrylic, watercolour
and ink) it is the people
who claim attention
rather than buildings,
which merely provide an
urban setting. He has
created a very powerful
and rather sinister effect
by playing with scale;
the foreground figures
on the steps dwarf their
surroundings.*

Composition
(Below) *Making a
finished drawing from
sketches or photographs
gives you more chance to
adjust reality. Ray Evans
sketches continually to
amass a store of visual
information, and when
he makes finished
drawings he often
combines elements from
several sketchbook
studies. His* Port Isaac *is
in pen and watercolour.*

or her face, but it is surprising how many people ignore the importance of the size of windows and doors, or the heights of roofs in relation to walls.

When drawing a designed building such as a historic cathedral or fine country house, such factors are naturally taken into account, because the grand scale of the building or the carefully planned balance of the architectural features are the principal attractions of the subject. But scale and proportion are always important, even when your subject is an old wooden barn or a higgledy-piggledy collection of cottages or town houses; these are the characteristics which will give your drawing a convincing "sense of place".

Relative sizes can be measured by holding up a pencil at arm's length and moving your thumb up and down it, but if you are drawing sight-size you can be more accurate by using a ruler to read off the actual measurements. Work out the height of the building in relation to its width, the proportion of wall to roof, and the number and size of the windows. Don't forget that the laws of diminishing size make the spaces between windows become smaller as they recede, as well as the windows themselves – this is a trap for the unwary. Be particularly

careful with doors, as they will look structurally impossible if they are too small, and bizarre if they are too large – doors are designed so that the average person can pass comfortably in and out without having to stoop or walk in sideways. People in a townscape give an indication of scale as well as creating a feeling of atmosphere, but make sure that the doors you put in can accommodate them.

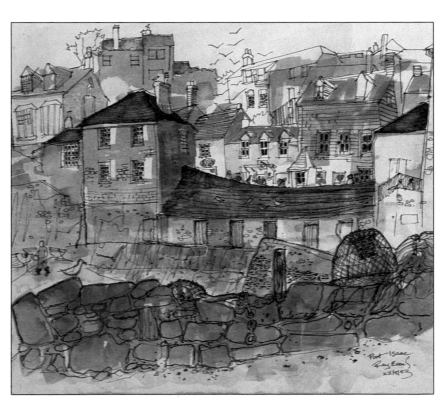

MIXED-MEDIA DEMONSTRATION

Karen Raney is an artist who enjoys experimenting with different media and different techniques, in both her drawings and her paintings. Her subject matter is as varied as her methods, but as a city dweller she is particularly interested in the challenge and stimulation of urban scenes. She uses photographs as a starting point when it is not possible to work direct from the subject – which can be difficult in towns and cities – but does so selectively, rejecting any elements in the photograph which she does not require for her composition.

1 *The artist intends to use a version of the sgraffito technique in combination with pencil and Conté crayon. She has begun by scribbling all over the paper with an oil bar, which is similar to a thick, soft oil pastel. Having drawn over this with Conté crayon, she now applies more in selected areas.*

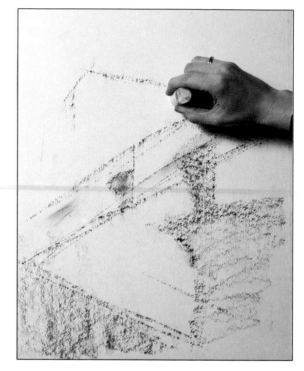

2 *The Conté crayon is smudged with a finger so that it mixes into the layers of oil bar beneath. The oil and the texture of the heavy watercolour paper have broken up the Conté marks, creating a nice soft effect.*

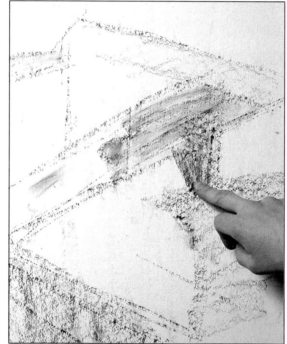

3 *Conté crayon is now inscribed more heavily over the first applications of oil and crayon. The drawing is kept loose and free at this stage, with the shapes evolving very gradually.*

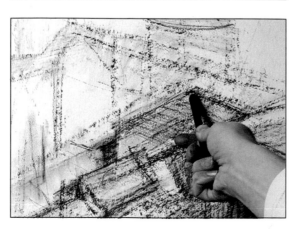

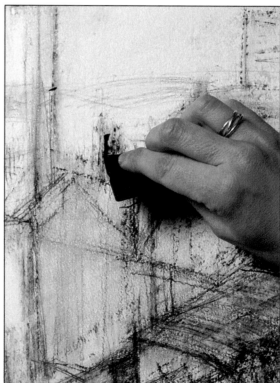

4 *The Conté has been applied quite heavily over the oil crayon, and the corner of a plastic card is employed, firstly to scratch into it and then to re-apply the resulting mixture of oil and Conté, which has become rather like paint.*

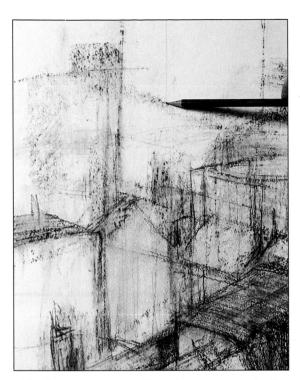

5 *The composition is allowed to emerge gradually, as the artist wished to establish the foreground before deciding on how many of the background buildings to include. She now uses a soft pencil to mark the side of a more distant building.*

6 *(Right) Detailed definition will be left until the final stages; concentration now is on the composition, the main perspective lines and the distribution of lights and darks.*

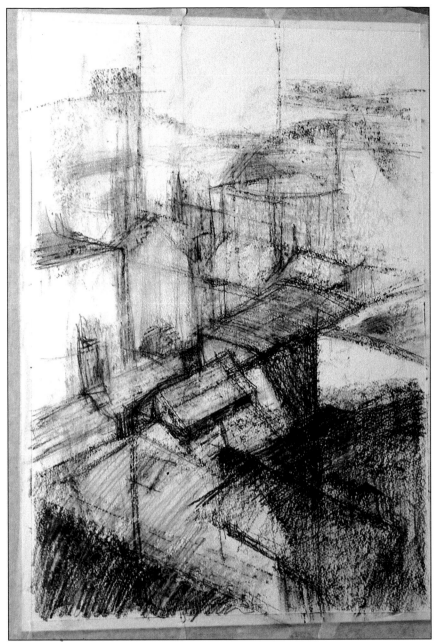

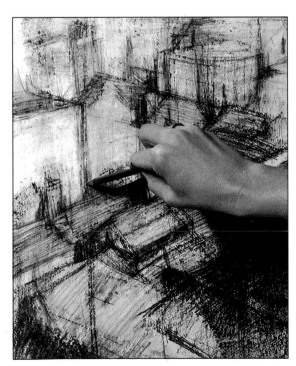

7 *Some of the lines are strengthened with soft pencil. In this photograph you can clearly see the effect of scratching and scraping with the plastic card, particularly in the foreground.*

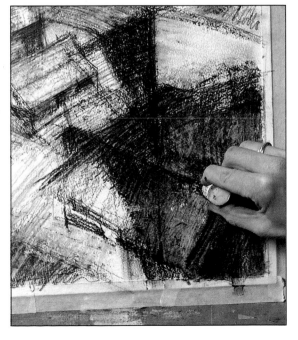

8 *A further application of oil bar again mixes with the Conté crayon beneath to produce a soft paste which can be manipulated and moved around.*

Continued ▷

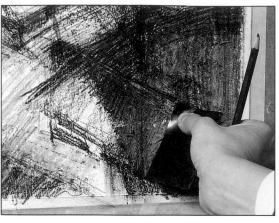

9 *The card is used to draw into the paste-like substance. The effect resembles brushmarks in a painting, with the corner of the card making a positive dark line.*

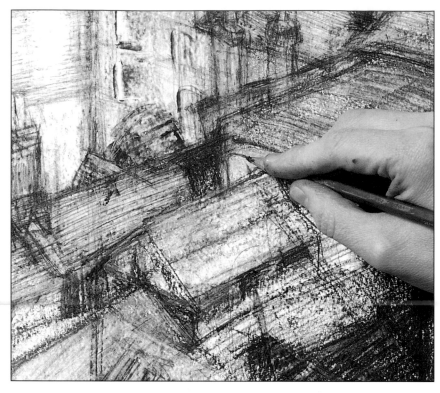

10 (Right) *The picture is sufficiently advanced for the artist to begin work on the details of the buildings, and here she uses a 2B pencil, applying pressure to bite through the thin layer of oil bar.*

11 *To suggest the texture of the building on the left, she has applied a further layer of oil bar and now draws into it, using the pencil lightly so that it only partially dislodges the oily underlayer.*

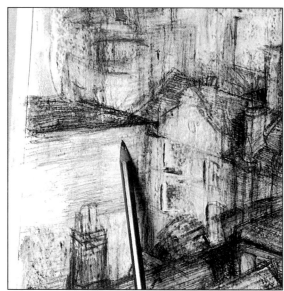

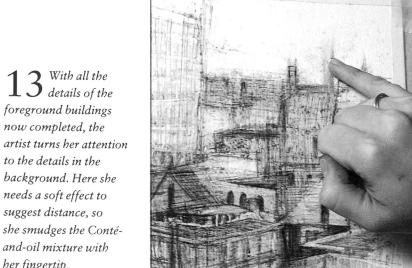

12 (Above) *A further hint of texture is given by painting over the lines of oil and Conté with white gouache. This also lightens an area which was previously rather too dark.*

13 *With all the details of the foreground buildings now completed, the artist turns her attention to the details in the background. Here she needs a soft effect to suggest distance, so she smudges the Conté-and-oil mixture with her fingertip.*

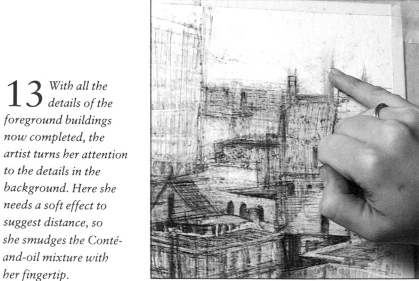

14 (Opposite) *The finished picture is not only an exciting evocation of a cityscape, it is also fascinating in terms of technique. The repeated layering and scraping of the Conté crayon and oil have produced a wonderful surface texture and density of tone which give the drawing something of the richness of an etching.*

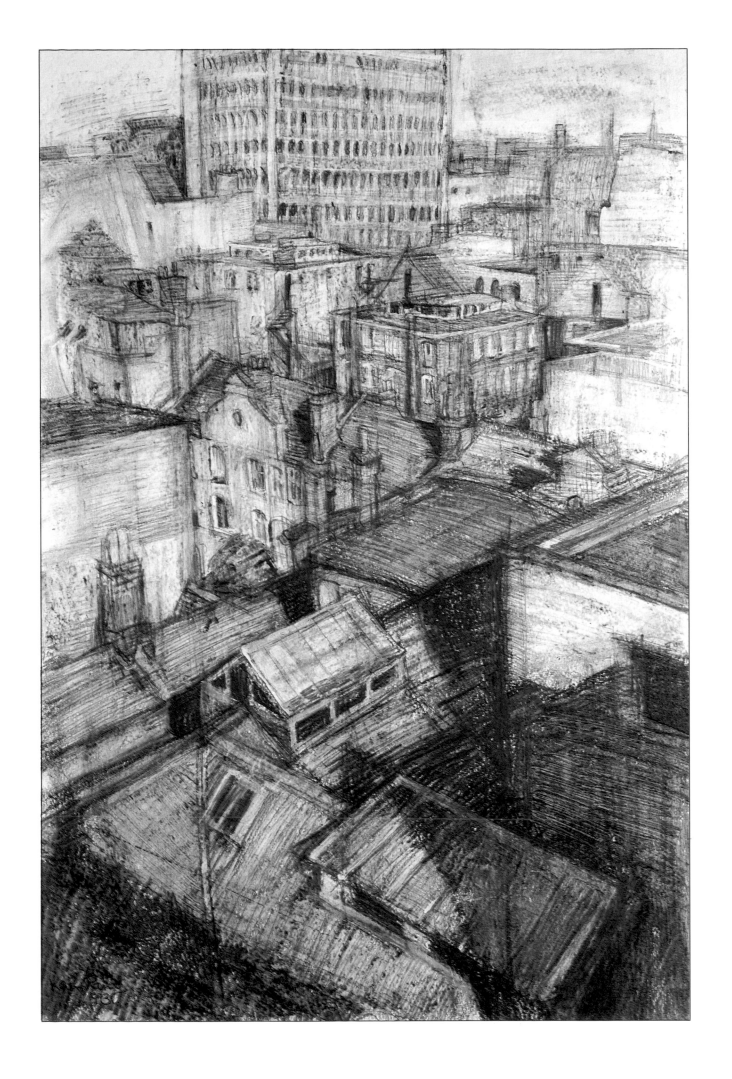

INDEX

PUBLISHER'S ACKNOWLEDGEMENTS

The Author and Publisher would like to thank the following companies for supplying materials used in the making of this book.

Cornelissen & Son Ltd
105 Great Russell Street
London WC1B 3RY

Daler-Rowney Ltd
PO Box 10
Southern Industrial Estate
Bracknell
Berkshire
RG12 8ST

Russell & Chapple Ltd
Canvas & Art Materials
23 Monmouth Street
London WC2H 9DE

Winsor & Newton
Whitefriars Avenue
Wealdstone
Harrow
Middlesex
HA3 5RH